THE HEALING MOMENT

7 Paths to Turn Messes into Miracles of Love

THE
HEALING
MOMENT

Dr. Donna Marks

BEYOND WORDS
Portland, Oregon

BEYOND WORDS

1750 S.W. Skyline Blvd, Suite 20
Portland, Oregon 97221-2543
503-531-8700 / 503-531-8773 fax
www.beyondword.com

First Beyond Words paperback edition April 2023

BEYOND WORDS PUBLISHING is an imprint of Simon & Schuster, Inc., and the Beyond Words
logo is a registered trademark of Beyond Words Publishing, Inc.

For information about special discounts for bulk purchases, please contact Beyond Words Special Sales
at 503-531-8700 or specialsales@beyondword.com.

Managing editor: Lindsay S. Easterbrooks-Brown
Editors: Michele Ashtiani Cohn, Bailey Potter
Copyeditor: Kristin Thiel
Proofreader: Sarah Heilman
Design: Devon Smith
Composition: William H. Brunson Typography Services

Manufactured in the United States of America

10 9 8 7 6 5 4 3 2 1

Library of Congress Cataloging-in-Publication Data

Names: Marks, Donna, author.
Title: The healing moment : 7 paths to turn messes into miracles of love /
   Dr. Donna Marks.
Description: First Beyond Words paperback edition. | Portland, Oregon :
   Beyond Words, 2023. | Includes bibliographical references.
Identifiers: LCCN 2022045510 (print) | LCCN 2022045511 (ebook) |
   ISBN 9781582708737 (paperback) | ISBN 9781582708744 (epub)
Subjects: LCSH: Self-actualization (Psychology) | Self-acceptance. | Mental healing.
Classification: LCC BF637.S4 M2285 2023 (print) | LCC BF637.S4 (ebook) |
   DDC 158.1—dc23/eng/20220930
LC record available at https://lccn.loc.gov/2022045510
LC ebook record available at https://lccn.loc.gov/2022045511

The corporate mission of Beyond Words Publishing, Inc.: *Inspire to Integrity*

This book is dedicated to everyone who has been on a spiritual journey and couldn't find their way. To those who must look everywhere before being convinced of the truth. And especially to those who have felt pain that brought them to their knees and instead of giving up, found their healing moment and accomplished what they came to do.

CONTENTS

PREFACE

In the following pages, I'm going to share some professional and personal stories with you. I'm very shy, and I'd rather walk a tightrope across a (deep) river gorge than reveal my personal life to strangers, but it isn't my mission in life to hide out in self-centered fear. I'm here to help people who want to find meaning and purpose in their lives. But first, we must remove the barriers that prevent that from happening.

If you're like me, you've done everything to seek happiness, and yet you've never discovered the promised "secret." Like many of my fellow travelers on a spiritual quest, I went through a process of elimination—church, Kabbalah, meditation, shamanism, spiritual books and gurus, seminars, twelve-step meetings, therapy, more therapy—but was unable to consistently apply it to daily life. My spiritual quest spanned a lifetime, but it took me hitting a second rock-hard bottom for me to realize the connection I sought was not external. The answer was much closer, and access to spirituality was profoundly simple. Once I was able to integrate all that I'd learned, I could sum up that information into the seven paths that took my life where I wanted to go: happiness. My perception that my life was a series of messes eventually turned into the realization that my life was a collage of miracles. Today, my life is filled with ongoing serenity. Even when I'm upset, I feel the stirrings of joy; it is my rudder and light.

Almost everything that brought me to this point seemed like a living nightmare. It took years, hard work, and a lot of suffering—mostly because of bad choices. But had it not been for *all* of life's experiences, I never would have asked a life-changing question: *Why doesn't God love me?* Nor would I have received the answer that catapulted me into an entirely different consciousness.

I was five years old when I first realized that my mind had two parts—a scared part and a loving part. My mom was kind and taught me a few values that became the fiber of my spiritual foundation. My favorite: "Heaven or hell is now. It's a choice depending on how you see things." As a child, I couldn't apply this idea to the pain I felt, but the seeds of its truth resonated with every fiber of my being.

My mom had her own wounds and was attracted to angry men. Her second husband, like her first, was abusive when drunk. One morning after one of his outbursts, I was flooded with emotions. Speaking to no one in particular, my five-year-old mind (the scared part) asked, *Why is this happening, and what's wrong with me?* A lightning response flashed through my mind (the loving part): *It's not your fault. He's sick.* My pain was instantly soothed by this truth and replaced with sorrow—for him.

But where did that second voice come from? Later, I realized that I'd had my first healing moment. It was in me but not of me. It wasn't until after many decades of searching for "how to get spiritual" that it dawned on me: I already had the spirituality that I'd so diligently sought.

Like many faulty communications, I failed to comprehend how spirit talk works. It's not always in words or signs, and sometimes it requires long stretches of waiting. Sometimes communication comes in silence, which doesn't mean "no;" it means "not now" or "there's something better for you." If I don't interfere, the answers will always come at the perfect time. And during those moments of waiting, I'm developing spiritual muscle—patience and faith.

As I moved further away from my five-year-old self, my life seemed to be a series of messes. Addiction and recovery, multiple failed relationships, a barrage of crises (cancer, deaths, fires, hurricanes, and family drama)—it seemed I couldn't get my head above water before another tidal wave struck. I finally gave up trying. I was the kind of person who generally walked a straight and narrow path, but when I screwed up, it wasn't a stumble. It was a jump off a hundred-foot cliff. After twenty-three years of sobriety, I consciously surrendered to the dark side and relapsed. Anyone watching would have cringed at my self-created horror show. *What in the world is she doing? What is she thinking? How could she do this to herself and others?*

Though my relapse was one of the worst mistakes in my life, I also experienced a sense of freedom. First, I'd been doing the right thing for all the wrong reasons. I complied and did what I was told to get sober, whether it resonated or not. I wanted to be a good girl, please God, and get the reward. And since it *seemed* like none of my good efforts yielded results, I grew angry. Now I was doing the wrong things for all the wrong reasons—rebellious little she-devil that I was—but at least what I was doing was real. I'd skipped the best part of my teens to get married and have a child, an effort to escape my dysfunctional family by starting my own. Now I was going to make up for lost time and have some fun.

The only problem was—like everything else I'd tried—it didn't work. And I couldn't blame anyone but myself for the outcome, not even God.

I'd run out of options: there were no more therapists, treatment centers, gurus, chanting around a bonfire, motivational speakers, or spiritual mountaintops. It all seemed like a waste; nothing had fixed me, and I was tired of trying. If my spiritual toolkit were to be constructed, it would have been the size of my house, and I could have retired on the money spent in my quest for truth. My chase only brought temporary relief, and it only seemed to patch together pieces of me, never unifying my whole being. Finally, I realized my spiritual journey was just another addiction. Still a ship without an anchor, drifting from port to port, I was searching but never finding what I truly wanted and needed.

I wanted nothing more than to have a stable life with family, friends, and a career. I loved my work as a therapist, but the rest eluded me. So even though the soil was tilled and the seeds had been planted, nothing grew because something was missing. I was desperate to connect with people, but too many betrayals (primarily my self-betrayals) had walled me in. Yes, there were real adversaries as well. Besides the before-mentioned disasters, there were hateful family members, disloyal friends, liars, and cheats. But my guilt kept me at their mercy. I simply couldn't crack the code and find my way out of the mental walls that imprisoned me. I wasn't stupid, but when it came to love, I was like a bird that repeatedly attacks its own reflection in a glass door, never realizing its error or self-destructive urge.

Trapped in the same patterns with family, friends, and lovers, I operated like an automaton that couldn't stop itself. I was living the personification of Sigmund Freud's quote, "A thing which has not been understood inevitably reappears; like an unlaid ghost, it cannot rest until the mystery has been resolved and the spell broken." I couldn't figure out under which spell I suffered. How could there be unlaid ghosts when I'd done so much personal work?

I'd lived my life up until this point believing I was flawed and guilty. Down deep, I didn't think I was good enough to have the life I wanted and thought I was too good for the life I was living. In recovery meetings, they call this an egomaniac with an inferiority complex. Sure, it was okay to achieve career success. But the bigger, bolder dreams of my heart were suppressed under the heavy load of shame—an unconscious, ever-pervasive sense of unworthiness. When I witnessed others get what they wanted, I'd be inspired. But when things didn't happen for me, my insecurities were reinforced. I imagined the benevolent creator, this God I had grown up with and always believed in, was withholding his gifts from me—the ultimate despairing, self-centered thought. My backward thinking would have to be reversed before I'd ever find peace.

My healing moment finally came when I asked the most important question of my life and received the truth. While having a temper tantrum with God, I demanded to know why he didn't love me. I'll tell you more about that later. For now, just know that the answer released me from the perception of being an unloved victim. I'd always thought love was a feeling and that this feeling was being withheld from me. I realized that love isn't a feeling at all. Love is an action.

This profound realization was incredibly empowering. For the first time, I was aware that I had the power to turn my life around. I realized every bad thing that had ever happened to me—all the missteps that had made my life a total heap of messes—could be put into perfect order. There was a gift in that struggle as well, as I saw that all the sad and painful events of my life had given me the ideal real-life education to help others recover from the same suffering. Rather than being a victim, I could use my experiences to fulfill my mission: to teach people how to love themselves so that they can achieve their own life's purpose.

INTRODUCTION

I am the light of the world. That is my only function.
That is why I'm here.
—*A Course in Miracles (Lesson 61)*

Most of us don't feel like the "light of the world." I certainly didn't. I do believe we are born with an inner light, but instead of fueling the light with love, it too often gets doused with negativity. If our true essence is not acknowledged from birth, if we're taught we're not good enough, the light is diminished. Then rather than shining forth into the world, we seek to obtain the light; always searching, never satisfied.

I searched my whole life for validation. Going from a high school dropout to earning a doctorate degree didn't change my self-esteem, nor did my lifelong education in areas of self-help and improvement. Going from rags to riches had little effect on my happiness because I saw the world in black-and-white instead of living color. Working with thousands of students and patients was gratifying, and it certainly gave me a reason to show up every day, but it didn't take away the gnawing feeling that there was a deficiency deep down inside of me. That low esteem started early in my life and was reinforced with a lifetime of misfortunes and sometimes tragedies—many of which were of my own doing. I didn't realize I wasn't here to do; I was here to be. To be light. To shine that light into the world.

♥

I didn't realize I wasn't here to do; I was here to be.
To be light. To shine that light into the world.

How does it happen that we don't know that we are the light that we seek?

It Starts at Birth

Children are born with an inner light that must be fanned with loving care. This is done by how they are treated, fed, and nurtured, as well as through effective role modeling. As long as there's enough of these essentials, a child feels loved.

♥

**Children are born with an inner light that must be
fanned with loving care.**

Adults shape children's concepts of themselves. The messages that are conveyed to kids are positive, negative, or a mixture of both. If there's too much negative input, the child's light diminishes. It's never gone; it just isn't accessed. When a child feels an abundance of love and acceptance, their light shines.

A safe family is a secure family, but caretakers don't realize that children can be more scared in their own homes than outside. Think about it. No one would give a baby heroin, alcohol, a whole chocolate pie, a cigarette, or tell them to do such foolish things to themselves or others. Yet babies watch other people do this all the time. "Do as I say and not as I do" only teaches confusion and hypocrisy—the internal compass goes haywire. Frequently I hear kids express how hard it is to watch their struggling parents—mood-altered, obese, or anorexic, coughing their lungs out, sex-crazed, hungover, or living in debt due to wasting money on addiction-related illnesses or reckless spending sprees. Yet, eventually, most of these same kids wind up just like their parents, if not worse. You can be the one who breaks out of this pattern.

One of my patients recalled that when she was young, she was so disturbed by her parents' constant parties that she posted No Drinking and No Smoking signs all over her house. Unfortunately, her parents didn't get the message. Eventually, when her conflicted emotions became too great, she drank the Kool-Aid too and embarked on her own get-out-of-reality campaign. By the time she was twenty years old, she was completely addicted to cocaine and alcohol and had been kicked out of college and arrested for disorderly conduct.

Let's not blame parents. They are intergenerational victims of a society that has lost its way, a global problem, not just limited to the US. In the past century, we've been subjected to deliberate brainwashing and hypnotic suggestions without our awareness through subversive messaging in information, technology, and the internet.[1] Subliminal advertising has implanted thoughts of food, sex, shopping, and more, causing us to want something without knowing why.[2] We've also been overtly bombarded with advertisements convincing consumers that their product is *the* way to feeling good.

We live in a world where success is measured by degrees, net income, and material possessions. There's no harm in wanting success and having nice things. Drive and ambition are the moving forces for creative developments and a nation's growth. But when the list of endless wants replaces human connection and purpose, the outcome is hell—a life devoid of love and meaning.

❤

Medication only masks feelings, and feelings aren't
something that can be erased like a chalkboard.

We're continually sold on fixing the empty, lonely, not-good-enough feelings that billions of us suffer. We're told it's better to take pills for the brain and the body than to understand the cause of our distress. Here's the thing, though: Medication only masks feelings, and feelings aren't something that can be erased like a chalkboard. Unresolved emotions take hold in the subconscious like a haunted mansion. Emotional wounds, like physical wounds, must be addressed. When ignored, they fester and seek to be constantly numbed by any means necessary.

Wake-Up Calls

It's time to face the facts. Our survival is at stake, and it's not for the reasons that we think. Global warming and deadly viruses aren't our greatest threats. Self-destructive, addictive behavior is at the bottom of most unnatural deaths. If you don't believe me, just do a little research. For example, take heart disease, the number one cause of death,[3] followed by cancer,[4] lung disease,[5] stroke,[6] and type 2 diabetes[7]—conditions caused mainly by toxins from alcohol, drugs, sugar, tobacco, and trans fats ingested to the point of causing permanent damage to the body's organs.

In other words, most of these illnesses are unknowingly self-inflicted by people who cannot stop drinking, eating, smoking, and ingesting poisons because they've become dependent on or addicted to them. But what do physicians do? Instead of labeling the problem, physicians tell patients to "cut down" on the behavior or prescribe them pills, as if addressing symptoms (instead of the real problem) will change anything. This type of help is a farce and causes people to live on a seesaw of temporary symptomatic relief. For a while they control their behavior. Then they lose control again. They never understand that their minds have been hijacked by substances that create cravings in the brain for more, more, more as the compass needle spins round and round.

Physical illnesses aren't the only thing killing us. Good mental health seems to be a thing of the past. The challenges of coping with unexpected trauma such as COVID-19[8] and endless wars have had lasting effects on those who suffer as well as those who are witnessing it through social media.[9] In 2020, of the 1.2 million people who attempted suicide worldwide, 800,000 succeeded.[10] And again, rather than address the causes of poor mental health, pills are often the solution.

Of the 77 million on psychiatric drugs in the US in 2020, over six million were children age seventeen and younger, with over 400,000 under age five.[11] The mental disorders pharmaceutic global market was $36 billion in 2020 and is expected to rise to $58.91 billion by 2031.[12]

Professionals in the mental health industry are sorely undertrained, and differentiating between mental health disorders and addiction can be tricky. Both can involve brain dysregulation resulting in anxiety, depression, and even psychosis. Not all people with mental health disorders have addictions, and vice-versa. Some have both disorders. It's essential to be able to identify and differentiate so that each condition is treated correctly.

Many people with addictions are diagnosed with mental health disorders, but after a period of sobriety, when the brain heals, the symptoms abate. The same is true of mental health disorders; some are temporary and due to emotional trauma, not a chemical imbalance in the brain. Prematurely subscribing medication, in either case, can blunt emotions and delay or even prevent emotional healing. Unfortunately, too many people are being lumped into mental health disorders and given medication whether they need it or not. I'm an advocate for psychotherapy, proper nutrition, and exercise as a first protocol, except in severe cases when a person's life is at risk.

While some mental health disorders are due to brain irregularities and require medication, too many people are assigned to the "pill mill." Just like medical doctors, psychiatric practitioners often give patients a "magic pill" instead of helping them heal trauma, change their coping skills, or stop behaviors that are abusing their brains, including a bad diet. Fortunately, more psychiatrists are prioritizing treating mental illness with psychotherapy, nutrition, supplements, stress reduction, exercise, and abstinence from chemicals (alcohol, drugs, trans fats, sugar, and any chemicals that adversely affect the brain).[13] How refreshing it would be if every pill prescriber suggested working through the pain instead of trying to cover it up. Don't get me wrong: we need physicians—they save lives on a regular basis. But we also need physicians to change the narrative from the treatment of symptoms to understanding their causes as well as prevention. Waiting until the teenage years and adulthood are too late, children must learn to honor their bodies and minds early on.

Many people treated for anxiety and depression suffer undiagnosed substance abuse problems. The correlation between substance abuse and poor mental health is clear.[14] I've worked with hundreds of people misdiagnosed with mental illness when they were simply substance abusers. Once the substance(s) was removed and the emotions were healed, the so-called mental illness vanished. Most experts agree that addiction is defined as continuing to do something despite repeated negative consequences. Yet we struggle to consistently realize that eating, drinking, gambling, pill-popping, porn watching, smoking, shopping, and video gaming with repeated negative consequences is addiction.

Let's talk about sugar. Many experts agree (myself included) that this substance is a highly addictive drug. Rutgers Center for Alcohol and Substance Use Studies provides an article that likens sugar to cocaine with a dopamine release, withdrawal, and relapse cycle, and identifies it as one of the key elements of obesity and type 2 diabetes.[15]

Bev provides an excellent example of someone who gained complete awareness of how the voice of fear had controlled her and then tackled a potential sugar addiction and turned it into a miracle of self-love.

Bev worked hard at maintaining good health. She walked three miles a day, followed a nutritious food plan, and didn't drink or smoke. Yet, she couldn't understand why she couldn't shake off an extra five pounds. Then, one morning she read an article in the *New York Times* about foods and beverages that misrepresented themselves as healthier but were actually addictive because of their high sugar content.[16] At first, she put the article down and told herself it was ridiculous.

But she struggled between the two voices she heard within. Bev was eating "low calorie" cereal or breakfast bars thinking it was a healthy choice. At the same time, it was dawning on her why she couldn't lose those last five pounds and why she often felt sluggish. She'd heard before that sugar was addictive like any other drug. She'd thought about giving up these foods but always succumbed to the fear that she would miss them too much.

Bev didn't ignore the voice that suggested she read the article again. This time, the light switched on, and she understood why she couldn't achieve her desired weight. Once Bev realized that she'd been obeying a harmful voice telling her she deserved a treat, she decided it was time to stop listening. Instead, she chose to love herself and look deeper at her behavior. She took out the box of cereal and looked at the sugar content. It was true; she was essentially eating a bowl of candy for breakfast.

Once she gave up the cereal and replaced it with free-range eggs and fresh fruit, her energy improved. She added a little exercise and lost the extra five pounds over the following few months. Bev embraced self-care and self-love. Love feels good—no guilt, no fear, only warm feelings of self-care.

♥

Love feels good—no guilt, no fear, only warm feelings of self-care.

Like the rest of us, Bev had two voices going on in her head, but she had to decide to switch on the light and to which voice she would listen. When Bev listened to the kind and gentle voice that helped her reach her goal, she turned her frustration and denial into victory.

Electronics may top the list of addictions. How often have you seen a family individually texting (or whatever) on their phones instead of relating to one another at the dinner table? It's disturbing to witness electronics used as babysitters for kids. When and where will children learn to relate to humans as well as they relate to technology? We should all heed Freud's teaching of the critical need for a child to form a secure attachment with a parent, which occurs through bonding. Bonding is the result of being held, seen, and heard as well as having the satisfaction of basic survival needs: food, shelter, and warmth. When these basics are missing, the search for what's missing is on. Eventually, we get so addicted to these poor substitutes that our brains are totally hijacked. We call it a habit, a problem, a weakness, or any other disguising, minimizing term. But how's that working for us? We've been taught that depression and anxiety should be eliminated at all costs. Remove all feelings! Close the door to the emotions that warn you something is wrong in your life! How misguided is that? Everyday stressors and feelings are part of life and need to be understood and healthily expressed lest we lose our ability to cope.

There's nothing logical about operating as if we're defective machines that need to be fixed. We're simply confused, adrift, hurting, and lost. We're not defective at all. We're just waiting to wake up, be affirmed by our own light, and heal. When you ignore your wake-up call, silencing it with pills or other addictive substances and behaviors, you succumb to assigning your life to someone else. In your attempt to feel better, you have turned off your light.

♥

There's nothing logical about operating as if we're defective machines that need to be fixed.

It's not my goal to convince people to face something they don't want to see. Instead, I encourage all those who want their minds back to reclaim them. It's time to learn how to love ourselves.

We've been programmed to seek satisfaction outside ourselves. As children, we are often taught to seek a certificate or trophy to reinforce success without being taught equal appreciation for a sense of pride in a job well done. Eventually, these awards are replaced with bank accounts and material possessions. Whoever has the most material gains is deemed the most successful. Consequently, instead of feeling fulfilled, we become more lost and learn to replace authentic gratification with addictive substitutes, like work and more possessions. When these cease to provide fulfillment, we move to alcohol, drugs, sex, power, and other endless replacements for self-love. We didn't intend to become this way. Once we tried something and got the reinforcement, we were hooked before we knew what hit us. All these things are substitutes for human connection.

Everything's at our fingertips, and we need only to push a button on a screen to get anything we want. Instant gratification has created an intolerance for waiting and has given us the impression the world is here at our service—always. When it's not, there's emotional fallout. I recently saw a news clip of a woman who was furious that social media was not suppressing a topic she didn't want to hear about. This woman expected the world to bend to her wishes rather than recognizing that a mentally healthy person copes with and self-regulates to life's challenges—not the other way around.

♥

If we replace unhealthy thoughts and actions with love, we can reclaim our light and our lives.

I'm not suggesting things were ever perfect; we're an evolving species. Each generation has more tools at its disposal for better parenting. Yet each generation seems to get busier, with both parents working, more single parents, kids in their rooms fixated on social media, and more dysfunction. There is less time for problem-solving, fun and games, structure, and life-skill guidance. Instead of abusing all the available distractions (alcohol, drugs, sex, and so on), healthy families make time for each other, including being present for their children's emotions. Children feel more secure when these needs are met.

If we replace unhealthy thoughts and actions with love, we can reclaim our light and our lives. But to do so, we must be willing to face what we're doing to impede our happiness. Our well-being depends on stopping the insanity under which we currently and often unconsciously operate. We must return to the natural state in which we were born.

Other Light-Dimming Sources

Most of the time, we don't realize how our minds are being conditioned. As children, we're lured into philosophies of family values and religion that shape and form our concepts about life and our roles within it. The goal is to provide a moral compass designed to lead us away from the pain of failure and toward safety and success.

Many of these dogmas contain wisdom and juicy bits of information that guide our circuitous path through life, but some of them create a sense of never being good enough. It's hard to find love when you've been taught your whole life that you're an evil sinner or a kid who can't get anything right. Setting unattainable standards for how to act and live—or the flip side of not enough structure and too much freedom—has created confused, neurotic human beings who can't stand being in their own skin. When we can't measure up to these conditioned expectations, we might seek pleasure in unhealthy ways. To cope, we settle for moments of empty glee in place of authentic joy.

That's not why you're here. Happiness is not something you get. It's the natural result of being connected to your inner light.

♥

Happiness is not something you get. It's the natural result of being connected to your inner light.

You Already Have the Light You Seek

When I was young, I was taught that God was an omnipotent being who loved us so much that he'd punish us for our sins if we strayed from his ways. The reward for obeying him was going to heaven, and the punishment was a sentence to hell.

I pictured an old magician way up in outer space holding a gigantic magic wand. He was so huge he'd cover an infinite amount of space. He had long, streaming white hair and wore a purple robe trimmed with gold and precious gems. His face had no revealing or penetrable expression, only a look of determination and conviction. If pleased with someone, God would spin his wand and grant the "good person's" wishes. For "sinners," the old man in the sky would use his magic wand to send rain, lightning, and frogs (or anything else) down on the evil sinner.

While these religious teachings conjured up scary images in my mind, I never believed a word about this loving, hateful God because it simply didn't make sense. A loving God kills his children and burns them in hell? Would I do that to my kids if they displeased me? Ridiculous!

Not only that, but it was also evident to my six-year-old mind that many other people didn't believe it either. After services, congregants were in such a hurry to leave that they'd practically run one another over in the parking lot just to get to the next destination. I saw religious people breaking the commandments all the time—extramarital affairs, lying, slandering, stealing, and all the other human "sins." No amount of guilt or fear stopped anyone from committing behaviors that would supposedly lead to eternal damnation. Clearly, they didn't believe their sins would send them to hell. Their distress-driven, unloving behavior had already put them there.

♥

We've been conditioned to confuse soothing ourselves with loving ourselves.

I'm not saying anything new here. There are tons of books and self-help programs that tell you to love yourself. But if you're like me, maybe you've read all the bestsellers and gone through the endless searching without ever finding anything real. And that's the big rub. We've been conditioned to confuse soothing ourselves with loving ourselves. Self-help can be another illusory fix. We have to reach a simpler but deeper level.

There's a higher consciousness that most people never tap into because they haven't learned how. Jesus talked about it, but few understood. His message was clear: Love God, love yourself, love one another. In other words, these acts are one and the same in that they're simply the act of loving. So simple, so misunderstood. And for those who do understand, there's a constant mental intrusion, like a nonstop staticky radio that blots out the voice of love.

What does your constant internal drumroll sound like?

What's for dinner? Time for candy, another cigarette. What's wrong with these damn drivers? Who is that idiot? I need a drink. How am I going to pay my mortgage? I'm hungry. What if I get caught? I need to refill my prescription. I'm bored. I hate my boss. She's hot. This sucks. I want another cookie. I'll never meet anyone. I hate it here. Are we there yet?

Rap, rap, rap, it goes. Nonstop.

If this is how your mind works, you are like everyone else who has been conditioned to chase after external validation and who hasn't accessed their light. Your mind will never stop talking, but you don't have to be at its mercy anymore. You can learn how to use the power of choice to decide to use your mind differently. The noise will never cease, but you're capable of listening to a different channel anytime you want.

♥

You can learn how to use the power of choice to decide to use your mind differently.

The healing moment is the point in time when you decide to turn on your internal switch and light floods into your consciousness. This *aha* experience will forever change you. You'll never again accept the dark, and you'll see the absurdity of how all the wrong things have ruled you.

There will be no more bumping into walls, fumbling through life, or wondering why things aren't working. You'll stop tripping over obstacles because you'll recognize them. You'll walk over, around, and in some cases right through them. Problems that used to get you down will become challenges that you embrace and enjoy. It feels good to experience the joy of freedom from a mind that has kept you in bondage.

Light removes the shadows. The big picture becomes clear, and the closets are free of boogeymen. As you learn to trust this guiding light, your confidence builds. You don't worry about the future. Instead, you embrace the excitement of today. That is all you have.

♥

> You'll stop tripping over obstacles because you'll recognize them. You'll walk over, around, and in some cases right through them.

You are the light of the world. Finding that light is the path to happiness.

Going Forward

As you read, you will notice many references to *A Course in Miracles*. *A Course in Miracles* was delivered to Dr. Helen Schucman, a self-proclaimed atheist, while she was employed as an assistant medical professor at Columbia University of Physicians and Surgeons, in 1965.[17] Shortly after Dr. Schucman expressed to one of her peers her feelings of disillusionment and her belief that "there must be a better way," she began to hear an inner dictation that said "this is a course in miracles," and she began to record what she heard.[18] Once Dr. Schucman commenced writing, a textbook, a workbook, and a teacher's manual were dictated to her and prepared for publication over the next ten years.[19] The *Course* was first published by the Foundation for Inner Peace, with over three million copies sold since 1976.[20]

While there are some criticisms of the *Course*, mostly religious, I suspect that the real problem for some people is that the power is taken away from institutions and put squarely with the mind of the reader. God is within, not to be delegated by anyone or anything else. Plus, the only fee for *A Course in Miracles* is the price of the book (a free PDF edition is available on the Miracle Distribution Center website),[21] and donations are voluntary as there are no large buildings or staff to support. There are study groups throughout the world that can be found by searching online for *A Course in Miracles* groups—most are free. Again, I'd like to emphasize that *A Course in Miracles* doesn't rely on an institution to teach you what you already know. Instead, it reconnects you to the inner voice that is your spiritual pipeline and God-given gift.

A Course in Miracles teaches the student how to remove the internal barriers to love. The *Course* defines a miracle as a "correction"; a change in perception from fear to love.[22] Rather than seeing lack, we begin to see abundance and opportunity for sharing. Instead of making someone wrong, we look past errors, face our own wounds, and see ways to heal ourselves and others. The goal is togetherness instead of separation. We accomplish all this by listening to the spiritual voice of love instead of the fearful voice of the ego.

In doing so, we can reclaim our actual state as beings who are here to share and receive love. *A Course in Miracles* is *not* spirituality 101. It's a course that requires your time, contemplation, and collaboration with others. *A Course in Miracles* is for people who are serious about spiritual growth. Unlike any other spirituality book, it treats the reader as a student and a teacher. There's a textbook and workbook with 365 lessons for daily learning along with a teacher's manual. The lessons help the reader to unlearn self-defeating thoughts and replace them with loving thoughts.

It has been my experience that twelve-step meetings and *A Course in Miracles* offer more wisdom than most other authorities on religion and spirituality. The second big difference: they're free. That doesn't diminish the cost or value of the decades I spent in psychoanalysis, including my thirty-year investment in personal and spiritual growth. It just took me a while to integrate everything. I spent far too much time searching and not applying what I'd learned. I hope to help you avoid the same missteps as you move toward your own healing moment.

Hitting the Switch

It starts with a first step.

Some people are never ready for this moment. If they don't want to come out of the cave, it's senseless to have a flashlight. The shadows in their minds keep them from facing fear, like an ominous cloud they constantly steer away from. Sunshine, greenery, and smiling faces can indeed be terrifying if you've never fully seen them. It's easier to remain comfortably blind and numb than to face the horror of a reality that demands change. In the cave, after all, you will always have free will, even if it causes you to self-destruct.

Maybe you're ready to emerge but have been struggling with making a change. The pseudo-comforts like food, pills, pot, the internet, a well-paying career you don't like, and virtual relationships aren't doing anything for you other than blocking your light. You think, *What would happen if I turned on the switch?*

You feel a slight stirring inside of you that catapults you forward. But like a child being drawn back into a candy shop, you can't stop yourself. You're torn. You can feel the light waiting to rush forward. You only have to flick on the switch.

A voice screams, *We can't give this up! We will be miserable outside of the cave!*

You stop. You think some more. You know it's true. You'll be giving up someone or something that you *think* you need, that you've depended on for so long to keep you from facing your pain.

So, you back away from the light, thinking, *Whew, that was close.* You retreat, wait, and continue to debate internally. Days, weeks, months, and years may slip away.

If this is you, then you're almost there. You're almost ready to emerge. Don't stop, and don't back up.

Some people are fortunate enough to confront their lives decisively. The moment they begin to ponder the possibility of a better life, the flicker of inner light disrupts their complacency. They let the vision of success gestate and take hold. For them, nothing will ever be the same. They no longer have to quit anything. They have transcended whatever held them back.

Don was a patient who reclaimed his light. By the time we met, he was like a piece of ripe fruit ready to drop off the tree and seed the ground with thousands of other fruiting trees. Blaming it on trying to please his wife, he claimed he suffered because he wasn't able to fulfill his dream career. When I asked him the real reason he wasn't following through with his plan for success, he admitted he was afraid of failure. No one ever had confidence in him. At his parents' insistence, he went to college, but he flunked out. Never finding his mission and purpose, he was haunted with the fear he wasn't smart enough to succeed at anything other than menial work.

We replaced that vision with another one. "Why not imagine you're successful beyond your wildest dreams?" I asked. "What would that look like?" At first, Don looked stunned, and then the light flooded in. Finally, he broke down, sobbing. "We'd have the kids, the house, financial freedom, and everyone would be proud of me," he said. "I'd be free." Once Don articulated his fears and replaced his nightmare vision with an image of heavenly success, the invisible steel bars became like paper straws and fell away. This was Don's healing moment, and the mess of his life transformed into the miracle of success. Once he believed in himself, his wife followed suit. Within a year, he had received his real estate license and earned an income beyond his wildest dreams, and soon after that, he learned a new baby was on the way.

♥

**Someone can guide you toward the light,
but you must be the one to turn on the switch.**

There is a light inside of you. Like the lamp on your desk, though, it doesn't come on by itself. That light is always there, waiting inside the bulb, waiting inside you, ready to provide you vision when you are in the dark. Someone can guide you toward the light, but you must be the one to turn on the switch. Once you do, light floods the room, and then you can see.

If you have found yourself in a miserable heap, frustrated with life, filled with self-loathing, and feeling powerless to change, it's time to consider a different path. There is another way.

There's no mess so great that it can't be cured with miracles. The miracle happens when you decide to reclaim your identity as a person who is here to share and receive love. But first, you must remove the barriers that have kept you in the dark and discover the paths to a life of success.

Are you ready to let your light flood the room? Are you ready to see?

♥

There's no mess so great that it can't be
cured with miracles.

What Follows

Most of what's shared in the following pages combines what I learned in *A Course in Miracles*, twelve-step meetings, and psychoanalysis. These teaching are integrated into concepts that are the seven paths to miracles. Each chapter provides examples from patients with whom I've worked as well as my own life experiences. At the end of each chapter are exercises to help you further integrate the readings. I would suggest you invest in a special notebook or diary to record your answers as well as any special insights you receive during the process. Take time to read and digest each chapter before doing the exercises. Don't rush to answer the questions either. It takes time to excavate buried memories, and the point is to heal the past, not brush over it. Give yourself plenty of quiet time so that you can digest what you're learning. Try keeping your notebook with you so that when a buried memory surfaces, you can write it down. Consider forming your own *Healing Moment* book group, which could meet for seven weeks (or more) to share in the healing process as you read. The more you invest, the more you will receive.

The following pages consolidate a lifetime of professional and personal learning and experience into seven paths. You can liken it to a map. Like me, you can start your spiritual journey without direction and spend a great deal of time wandering around. No harm done, just time spent learning the same concepts instead of applying the knowledge. Or you can follow the map to reach your destination quickly and then travel around along the deeper paths in a more empowered state. I share these paths with you in the hopes that your journey will be shortened and that you will now have the choice to replace life's inevitable pain with healing moments and miracles.

The Healing Moment attempts to combine the concepts of *A Course in Miracles* with psychology and spirituality in a simplified manner. Once you learn the seven paths, you will be able to switch from a reactive incapacitated state to a clear mindset that leads to loving solutions.

Chapter 1

FIRST PATH: THE VOICE OF LOVE

The Most Important Guidance You Will Ever Receive
Is Deep Within

You must choose to hear one of two voices within you.
—*A Course in Miracles (Chapter 5, II)*

There are two voices in your head.

One voice is gentle and quiet. The other voice is loud and convincing. One of them is whispering in your ear to wake up. The other is telling you to stay asleep.

The loud voice is the one we listen to most of the time. That voice is called *fear*. It came about when painful things happened and pushed out the voice of love. Like when someone you love is pulling away, they won't communicate, and the future is uncertain.

I'm not talking about terror. Terror is when something terrible is happening: an accident, a death, a disaster, a real threat to your life and well-being.

Fear is different.

The voice of fear is where messes happen. It's constantly telling us what to do—and it's usually wrong. "Yeah, scream at that person who pulled out in front of you." "Don't let go." "Get even with the woman who hurt you." "Go ahead and steal a few dollars, no one will notice." "Eat that other piece of cake—you deserve it." "Have the extra drink." "Spend the money." "Make a bet." "Lie to your partner." "Do whatever makes you feel good—

1

who cares if it upsets someone? You're always doing something for everyone else. It's time for you."

Fear, being the coward it is, hides under anger and guilt. It forces you to ruminate and obsess over the conflict and never gives you peace.

♥

. . . anger should never be suppressed. It's an emotion that must be converted to loving communication.

Guilt is the master manipulator's tool. It makes you feel deficient and unforgivable. It tells you that any problem can be fixed with more exertion, more self-control. But guilt rarely stops someone from doing something they really want to do. They'll do the act and then feel paranoid that God (or someone else) will punish them, but it doesn't stop them from doing it again. In fact, it has the opposite effect. The more someone tries to control something they think they enjoy, the more they want to keep doing it.

Anger makes others feel guilty and unworthy. While it's normal to get mad at someone, telling the person off will only cause them to shrink away. You might get what you want from expressing your anger, but it won't win friends and will surely create resentment. Eventually, anger blows everyone away. But anger should never be suppressed. It's an emotion that must be converted to loving communication.

Fear sweeps everything into a big pot of chaos so that you stay too bewildered and confused to sort things out. It justifies all unhealthy behaviors. It avoids solutions at all costs.

Instead of being responsible for ourselves, we blame God or surrender our power to other people who become our higher power. And being "evil sinners" has led us to the faulty conclusion that it's not okay to make mistakes. This helpless-victim consciousness means we never have to face our fears and lets us put all the responsibility for our failures or successes on God.

Even worse, when someone hits an emotional bottom and sincerely seeks enlightenment, they often find themselves on a path to disappointment and disillusionment paved with hustlers disguising themselves as healers. The "healers," to whom they've turned over their will, lives, trust, and resources, might not deliver the peace they seek. When the quick fix doesn't work, there's no one there for continued support. Sometimes, instead of finding truth and spirituality, they find themselves in the bedroom, withdrawing money from the bank, or at some isolated location serving a master who is far sicker than they are.

Jim Jones was an extreme example of a spiritually sick psychopath. In 1977, Jones took his followers from the Peoples Temple in Indiana to Guyana to set up a commune in Jonestown, and while under investigation for alleged abuse of his congregants, he ordered a mass suicide resulting in the death of almost a thousand adults and children.[1] Later, the world also witnessed the horrifying news of Catholic priests sexually abusing young boys and then stonewalling the truth, resulting in over $4 billion in settlements to the victims worldwide.[2] In the US, over 5,300 priests in 51 states have been accused of sexually abusing children,[3] resulting in Catholic church payouts of over 3 billion dollars to the victims.[4] A man known as John of God in Brazil, a world-renowned faith healer, was arrested several years ago for over three hundred cases of sexual assault on women.[5] I've witnessed numerous exploitations at various spiritual events, some by renowned motivational speakers. Anyone can search the internet and find endless reports of cult founders, ministers, gurus, and other spiritual leaders who cross the line and violate the sanctity of their followers.

Justine got hooked on a motivational leader. When she left the first event, she felt high and signed up for another event. This time she upgraded her seating to the front row where all the millionaires sat. During the event, there was a meditation on releasing sexual energy. That night she was in bed with one of the front-seaters. Once she returned home and didn't hear from him again, she began to feel uncomfortable. She'd turned herself over to something that influenced her without fully realizing what she'd done. Has Justine consulted with her inner voice, she might have made a more conscious decision instead of floating into a situation that she later regretted.

Even in churches and recovery meetings where people are desperate for help, they often find predators instead. This is not the norm, but as they do anyplace else, predators exist there, too. People who have a childhood history of being violated are more susceptible to being victims.

It's important to listen to your inner guide and if unsure, ask around before making any decisions. If someone is trying to get something from you, stay away. Everyone in the recovery meetings knows they are not supposed to approach newcomers for sex, money, or personal gain.

Often, these unhealed healers, as I like to call them, aren't at fault for their mistakes. Some are merely reenacting what they were taught. Others are too sick or exhausted to do any better, or they cannot access the voice of love that would honor the vulnerability of the people who worship them.

♥

Your healing moment is when you realize who you are
and why you're here.

There's no reason to condemn all spiritual leaders: we've all had our blind spots, and the journey takes time. Some are genuine and capable. And there's nothing wrong with guiding people to do what parents, teachers, and other leaders have failed to do for them. The purpose of any guide is to help you find your way to truth. The goal is for you to find your mission and purpose. Your healing moment is when you realize who you are and why you're here. But we must not be swept away and turn our power over to people who aren't spiritually fit or have motives other than our well-being. The greatest teacher is within, and this is the relationship that is the most important to honor and obey.

Back to our two voices. You've probably heard the softer, gentler voice say something like, "That might not be a good idea." And you've likely charged ahead and ignored it. That voice is often referred to as our conscience, part of our intuition that is our internal spiritual navigation system. Its purpose is to help us discern right from wrong. But our conscience is something we all have to live with and is merely the doorway to a deeper voice that goes beyond just telling us to follow the rules. That voice comes from our spirit and is called *love*. Accessing the voice of love is voluntary. When you're under its guidance, the focus isn't on external rules. The emphasis is on making choices that produce self-love and self-respect.

The voice of love is where miracles happen. We are not robots moving from one input to the next. We are here to share and receive love, and every one of us has an internal place where love resides. This perfect human navigation system reminds us to approach life from the position of love instead of fear. When we listen to that voice, we make the best choices and live the way we're designed. But we don't realize we're often tuned in to the louder voice of fear. We've been told we need to watch out, cover our backs. We've been told not to feel too much. To avoid mistakes. We are constantly bombarded with messages that to be okay, we need something other than what we have or who we are. As a result, we become dependent on outside sources for fulfillment, always chasing and never reaching the center, which starts with ourselves. The emptier and lonelier we get, the harder we try to cover up that expanding void through artificial means. The voice of fear guides us into dissatisfying careers, bad marriages, poor decisions, and addictions—digging our own personal hole into hell.

Even though you could be much happier if you gave up the thing that's harming you, the loud voice convinces you to keep right on. It tells you misery is certain without your fix of choice. You struggle, knowing you shouldn't partake in things that threaten your health and happiness, but fear's cunning and convincing arguments override the voice of love.

"Go ahead," it repeats. "You deserve this."

And even though you know you shouldn't, the voice of fear convinces you to go ahead. But what happens when you say yes, again, despite your better judgment? That same voice condemns you for doing the very thing it just talked you into doing. Did you catch that? Fear follows pressure with blame. "You're a loser. Why didn't you listen to what your friend told you?" "Why did you lie? Now you're really in trouble." "You stupid idiot, why did you drink last night? You knew you would feel like crap today." "You deserve to be fat; you ate the whole damn cake." "You'll get caught one day, and then you'll get what's coming to you." "Good move telling him off. When will you ever learn to keep your mouth shut?"

That's right. The voice of fear commanded you to do something and then doubled down on its fear-based attack when you followed its very advice.

Without even realizing what your own mind has done, you've acted and then reacted without consciously knowing you're the puppet of a self-destructive internal voice that's out to sabotage you. Why? Because the voice of fear evolved from old wounds. Then those wounds need to be constantly medicated with anything that makes them magically disappear—alcohol, busyness, drugs, excitement, gambling, shopping, sex, and so on. The voice of fear tells you that if you don't get your fix, you will feel awful. It never tells you to deal with that underlying malaise; it just keeps covering it up.

But fear can't serve as an effective compass because the needle aimlessly spins around. Its only function is to create as many messes as possible. Of course it never cleans them up but instead heaps on more dirt until you're buried so deep, you're too exhausted even to try to get out.

Remember, I'm not talking about a real threat. I'm talking about the imaginary scenarios that fear produces. Things like "I should go ahead and marry this person even though I don't feel in love with her. I'm forty years old, and I'll never meet anyone better." "I'll just sneak these new clothes into the house, and my spouse will never know the difference." "I haven't used drugs in over a year—I'm sure one hit won't hurt anything." "I'll just blame my lack of weight loss on the diet and continue sneaking sweets when no one is looking." "I know my spouse is having an affair, so I'm going to do whatever I want." The fear underneath all these choices creates a bigger mess. At any point in time, a person could ask, "Why am I doing this? What am I trying to avoid? What is driving my behavior?" Those questions would prompt healing, remove the fear that drives the behavior, then fill that consciousness with self-love.

The Origin of Fear

Caretakers make mistakes ranging from mild to severe. It does no good to make parents feel guilty, but it is good to heal wounded relationships. I've worked with many parents and children who were able to talk about the past, mourn it, and make peace with each other. I believe parents look back and regret how they raised their children, and that's why many of them make such loving grandparents. But making amends directly is more healing for everyone. Regardless, no matter what happened in your child-hood, you can heal. But first, you must understand how to free yourself.

For every scary event, starting with our earliest memories, an invisible brick is added to an imaginary wall around our hearts. For every hurtful moment, life feels less and less safe. If we'd been able to get the pain out by crying and sharing the pain, it would have dissolved into the healing moment of love and forgiveness. We wouldn't be afraid of getting hurt again because we'd know it hurts for a little while, and then we get over it. But when the pain is suppressed, fear makes us cautious and hyper-vigilant. But it doesn't protect us at all; it just put us in an invisible prison, sepa-rated from love. Fear also tells us to avoid our feelings, that there's nothing worse than showing your pain, so more bricks are added to the wall. We'll do almost anything to avoid those feelings by the time we're adults. But fear has another trick up its sleeve—boredom, or fear of nothing to do. Fear keeps us distracted by suggesting one pleasurable experience after the next. These experiences usually produce guilt or frustration, more bricks for fear to hide behind, more justification for distraction, and the compass keeps spinning.

Can you relate to this cycle? If so, you don't have to do it anymore.

To find freedom, there's a word that must be banned from your vocabulary: *anxiety*. Anxiety makes you feel uncomfortable, and that dis-tress then deters you from doing something that you need to do. Just the thought of facing what's disturbing you increases the anxiety.

Anxiety is simply another word for *fear*. Fear (packaged as anxiety) seems like the perfect reason to take benzodiazepines (Valium, Xanax, Halcion, Ativan, and Klonopin, etc.) to calm down, despite these drugs being dangerous and addictive.[6] Between January 2019 and June 2020, they caused over seven thousand deaths and 17 percent of all overdoses in the US.[7] In 2019, *Psychiatry Services* reported that 30.6 million adults were prescribed these drugs, and 5.3 million misused them.[8] In 2021, the National Institute of Health reported a worldwide increase in benzodiaze-pine prescriptions due to COVID-related anxiety.[9]

♥

To find freedom, there's a word that must be banned
from your vocabulary: *anxiety*.

Here's the typical scenario for getting hooked on benzos. You go to a physician because you're feeling stressed or anxious or are suffering from obsessive-compulsive disorder. You are told you're suffering from anxiety, a brain disorder, or some other "chemical imbalance" that you can't help, and you need drugs. The doctor knows best, right? So, you take the pills, and they work. You feel relaxed, and life seems better.

One big problem, though: you haven't solved a thing. You still have anxiety, albeit anxiety that's being masked by a pill, but now you have a pill dependence too. This monkey on your back will most likely invite other monkeys, and trust me, they aren't likely to voluntarily leave their new residence.

♥

It's never too late to have a happy adulthood.

Through attention to language, though, we can take power over this oppressor. Distance yourself from the idea of anxiety as a clinical condition and remember that it's most often simply fear. Anxiety can feel foreign, heavy, and frightening. Fear, however, we know is a normal part of being human. By recasting the idea of anxiety as fear, you will be empowered to normalize and overcome what are normal feelings. But what if your distress tolerance is terrible? What if no one prepared you for life's discomforts when you were young? It's never too late to learn. It's never too late to have a happy adulthood.

Once you realize your real enemy is the voice of fear, identify that voice, and normalize the distress it causes you, you can take back control. You can observe the conversation in your head without making it real. You can hear but no longer listen to the blaring voice because you're now armed with the truth of its one and only mission: to disable you. But ignoring that voice isn't enough. You must teach yourself how to ask for help and listen to the softer, gentler voice. Just as you learned how to get up and get dressed in the morning, brush your teeth, hold your fork, throw a ball, drive a car, make a significant financial decision, or anything else, you must now learn how to listen to the soft voice, the voice of love. You learn to walk through your fear and gain power.

I've had the honor of working with people who have gone so far into the hellhole of addiction, anxiety, or depression that it seemed like they'd never get out. Like me, they'd been to many therapists, psychiatrists, and healers, only to find a web of formulas and prescriptions spun around their very souls. We've all experienced pills, the quick fix du jour, or magic formulas that didn't work. We became unconscious as our lives ticked on without our full presence.

When these patients come in for therapy, they aren't expecting to work at getting better; they want a pill or any other method that doesn't require effort. Many psychiatric disorders are caused by bad habits such as poor nutrition or substance abuse. For example, low blood sugar from improper nutrition can cause emotional volatility. When we examine diet and lifestyle, patients often respond with comments like "I can't eat healthily. I don't have time. It's easier to grab and go." "What's wrong with a few drinks at night? How else can I get rid of the stress?" "I know I eat too much sugar, but it's my only treat." "My doctor says I'm clinically depressed, and it's a brain disorder, and I have to take these pills." When a brain has been abused by poor diet, substances, or trauma, it becomes disordered. But given proper care and time to heal, it can return to its natural healthy state.

Is all fear bad? Of course not. You need to be scared when your life is in danger. In a life-threatening situation, fear is good. Your body releases chemicals to make it stronger to defend itself. But living in a state of high intensity all the time is toxic and will wear you down mentally and physically.

We Have to Face the Pain

Resistance to change can be like molasses in January. As a therapist, I can show patients the way, but I can't make them see what they don't want to face. I must wait until they are ready to thaw. I never give up on them. I love them and have faith in the power of their spirits to melt away the walls of fear. There is nothing more fulfilling than seeing people rise from their living graves and return to their life's purpose. To see fear and compulsive behavior replaced with meaning and joy is one of the greatest gifts any human can witness.

One patient, Carla, took more than a decade to face her addiction. After coming off a lifetime of alcohol and opiates, then addressing her childhood pain as a sex-abuse survivor, she surprised me when she said she no longer needed her Xanax, and her physician was weaning her off. "I'm not afraid anymore," she told me. "I used to be afraid to go into an elevator or be around people I didn't know. I couldn't go anywhere. Now, I don't need anything else to function. All those vices were burdens. I'm free. I see and think more clearly. I've never been so happy."

Another patient, Sherry, wanted to come off her antidepressant. Twenty years earlier, when she confided in her physician that she was unhappy in her marriage, instead of recommending therapy to face the cause of her emotional state, he wrote a prescription. Now she had two problems: a dissatisfying marriage and a drug dependency. Even though she slowly weaned off the medication, the withdrawal was brutal. She couldn't sleep. She suffered constant agitation. She felt like she was in the twilight zone. And she was.

Even though it took more than a year for her brain to re-regulate and for her to find the "happy-go-lucky" girl she was before her depression, she braved her way through the pain and darkness and finally succeeded. She now feels the self-love that had been missing since she was that happy little girl.

We aren't here to self-medicate, suffer, or settle for a life we don't want. We are here to share and receive love, to play, and to contribute to our life's mission and purpose.

The voice of love is where you will find every healing moment. No matter how many messes you've made of your health, life, or relationships, this is the way to turn all messes into miracles.

While this book is about finding your voice of love, let's be clear that change requires personal effort; there's no quick fix. It takes a commitment of time, openness, and willingness to learn how to choose love over fear. You must be coachable and say, "I don't know what I'm doing wrong, and I'm willing to learn." Don't quit before the miracle. It might be challenging to learn new behaviors, especially those that aren't comfortable and require digging deep within, but you are worth the effort.

Learning to love yourself means replacing bad habits with new, healthy thoughts and actions. When you've lived in an immediate gratification mode, it feels unnatural to grow. All seeds take time to grow and harvest, though. Impatience only serves up a platter of failures, and you are not here to fail.

---------------------------- ♥ ----------------------------

**Impatience only serves up a platter of failures,
and you are not here to fail.**

I can't tell you how many people have sought advice, received guidance, and dismissed the diagnosis and treatment plan altogether. For example, when I point out to a patient that their life is unmanageable because of the money and time spent on a "bad habit," they often reply, "No, my problem isn't drinking, sex, or gambling—you just don't understand me." If I point out that they might have it backward and that they might not understand addiction or themselves, they become indignant. "You probably think everyone has an addiction," they often say. At that point, I might suggest they consider stopping those harmful behaviors and replacing them with actual loving behaviors, just to see if it might work. For example, instead of doing drugs at night, go to the gym, get a massage, take a hot bath, or take up a hobby. Some people are receptive. Some are not.

Chris had been addicted to alcohol and drugs but sought help from a support group and managed to get off these substances. His life improved immensely, and he was able to finish school and get a good job. There was just one glitch. He didn't think of Valium as a drug because his doctor prescribed it for anxiety, and he was afraid to give it up. He used it every time he felt nervous instead of getting to the roots of what made him feel that way. He remained stuck in his romantic relationships and couldn't make commitments. His family, also dependent on various substances, did not support him in stopping Valium. Taking pills was a deeply ingrained pattern in the family, and the thought of living without them was a severe threat to the system. But the Valium was a curtain that kept out Craig's light and held him in fear. He was so close to the miracle of love, but he simply couldn't cross the finish line.

All too often, a person is reenacting a parent's behavior, and anyone breaking free of the system is a threat. When a person's life is working well enough despite sorrow and illness, they can't see how much better it would be by facing hard truths. Any single person in a family who chooses to listen to the voice of love could turn their life around, often positively affecting the entire family. Having an addiction is like turning the volume down on the radio. It doesn't allow you to hear unless you choose to listen.

No magician in the sky is going to fix everything for you or punish you for your mistakes. But the voice of love will guide you along your journey toward your vision and dreams. Whether you're in a life crisis or fail to achieve a specific goal, you might be operating under the voice of fear. Perhaps it's time to consider that there's a switch in your mind—you can turn it on and shed some light on your problem, no matter how big or how small.

The most important guidance you will ever receive is deep within. Listen to the voice of love—that is your path to miracles.

Your conflicts and problems might be with yourself or others, but you can have a healing moment that will replace all messes with miracles no matter what the mess. But first, you must be willing to see things differently. The following pages can help you take back the authority you have given others and restore it to yourself. Are you ready?

The most important guidance you will ever receive is deep within. Listen to the voice of love—that is your path to miracles.

Your Healing Moment Exercise 1: Recognizing Your Two Voices

The following exercise will help you to get better acquainted with the two voices in your head—love and fear—and to strengthen a connection with your loving voice.

1. Are you aware that you hear conflicting messages in your mind?

   _____

   _____

2. When did you first feel afraid? Describe how that feeling grew over time.

   _____

   _____

3. Give an example in which you felt conflicted.
   a. One voice told you:

   _____

   b. The other voice told you:

   _____

4. Which voice was based in fear, and which one was coming from love?

   _____

   _____

5. To which voice did you listen?
    a. Were you happy with the result?

    _____

    _____

    b. Why or why not?

    _____

    _____

6. Do you feel you've been living in the dark?

    _____

    _____

    _____

7. Are you ready to listen to the voice that will let in the light?

    _____

    _____

    _____

Three-Step Exercise for Fear

When fear (aka anxiety) seizes you, do these three things:

1. Close your eyes.
2. Embrace the feelings.
3. Consciously breathe and wait until the feelings pass and you feel at peace.

This simple practice on a regular basis will move you through your fears toward love.

Chapter 2

SECOND PATH: CONTROL

The Most Important Person You Will Ever Control Is Yourself

You have been fearful of everyone and everything.
—*A Course in Miracles (Chapter 2, VII)*

Do you think you are at the mercy of other people? Does it ever feel like you are a puppet being pulled by someone else's strings? Have you ever considered that you might be allowing this to happen? Have you ever thought about taking back your power and control, no matter how uncomfortable you feel or how much resistance you face?

Or maybe you've been the one in charge of others. Did you decide you'd never trust anyone at all? If everyone would just behave the way you want (whether they know your wishes or not), you'd be just fine. But then, when they don't follow your (unexpressed) likes and dislikes, you feel angry and disappointed; they are supposed to know the rules. Alas, if only everyone had the same rules.

♥

Have you ever thought about taking back your power and control, no matter how uncomfortable you feel or how much resistance you face?

Opposing Sides

As I write, the world is split, with each side trying to control the narrative on numerous issues from politics to vaccines and other hot topics. Depending on where you get your information, you are influenced. Each side believes they are equally correct despite their vastly different perspectives. But we are at the mercy of what we read. If we are not subjected to both sides of an argument, we have a limited point of view. When there's an intolerance to discussing divergent points of view, we have tunnel vision. Fear has invaded our minds to the point that we have become vulnerable to believing information that may or may not be correct. Closed minds can't access facts. It's easier to take things at face value than dig for the truth. This is the wrong form of control.

♥

**We should always attack the problems, not one another.
This is the way of love. Love never tries to control.**

Instead of coming together to problem-solve, the opposing point of view is deemed crazy, evil, and unpatriotic. There is an attempt to make others feel guilty for who they are and what they believe—the wrong form of control. This is the way of fear.

We should always attack the problems, not one another. This is the way of love. Love never tries to control.

♥

**We can explore and think for ourselves,
and we should utilize that freedom.**

What are we afraid of? The truth? Having to change our mind about something that we've already decided upon? What if we believe something that seems entirely logical but could be totally wrong? We can explore and think for ourselves, and we should utilize that freedom.

Of course, you can exercise control over others and even make them do what you want, but you will never control how they feel about you. You'd be much wiser to rein in that energy and exercise control over yourself and how you feel about yourself and your own beliefs.

This doesn't mean withdrawing into the silent role of a victim, however. A powerful voice speaks the truth but always with love.

♥

A powerful voice speaks the truth but always with love.

Blame vs. Taking Responsibility

Most people go through life projecting their problems onto other people, places, and things. This is learned behavior. It's called the blame game. "It's not my fault" or "it's your fault" is the standard refrain. Thoughts like "I got ripped off," "God didn't want me to have it," or "it is what it is" place the responsibility for winning elsewhere and don't allow us to be responsible for our own destiny. This type of rationalized blame keeps us in a state of victimhood. It's the mentality of disappointments and failure. Furthermore, the idea that *everyone else needs to change* is futile. Being a victim is a choice.

♥

Being a victim is a choice.

Unfortunately, most of us are victims of our own paranoid thoughts. Rather than using our less-desirable experiences to learn and grow, we buckle under the weight of disappointment. We think we failed because we weren't good or smart enough or because we're being punished for something cosmically. You don't have to be a rocket scientist to succeed, though, and God doesn't have time to worry about things not going your way personally. He gave us the tools, and we need only utilize them. If one thing doesn't work, try another. If you make an error in judgment, learn from it, and be wiser next time. There's always a next time.

_____ ♥ _____

**If you make an error in judgment, learn from it,
and be wiser next time. There's always a next time.**

_____

Some of us believe if we miss an opportunity, we're screwed for life. There is no shortage of chances, and we aren't punished for missing them. We may punish ourselves by losing faith in our abilities, but that's choosing fear, not love.

_____ ♥ _____

**When we succumb to our fears instead of working
beyond them, we become susceptible to an
addictive mindset.**

_____

When we succumb to our fears instead of working beyond them, we become susceptible to an addictive mindset. We start thinking that the thing we desire is supposed to happen right now, without fail. When we don't get immediate gratification, we fall into despair or agitation and risk self-medicating. Some people drink or take pills to ease the internal unrest.

Others develop anxiety, phobias, and obsessive-compulsive disorders, as if being nervous or paranoid will atone for their faults and make good things happen. All these conditions are simply unresolved fear. We are trying to fix the inside by outside means. It will never work.

I Need You but Not Too Much

Control issues start in childhood. The wrong amount of control can result in obsessive-compulsive disorder (the need to control everything), fear (disguised as anxiety), insecurity, and depression. Over- or under-managed children will unconsciously bump up against the same walls throughout life. If parents exercise too much control, the child learns to feel inadequate and either dependent on or resentful of others' management of them. Or they might tend to be a people-pleaser for fear of criticism. They haven't learned to find out for themselves and develop trust in their instincts. When a parent doesn't provide enough control, the child has difficulty with boundaries and is too easily influenced by others. There needs to be a balance of guidance and freedom in child-rearing. This teaches children how to think for themselves and to respect others. Children should be provided with the information they need to know for their safety and then encouraged to trust their instincts. If not, they grow up disavowing their intuition and lose their way.

♥

... there are times in our lives that throw up
impenetrable roadblocks or unexpected losses or
catastrophes. But even these events can be used
for betterment and spiritual growth—
opportunities for healing moments.

Of course, there are times in our lives that throw up impenetrable roadblocks or unexpected losses or catastrophes. But even these events can be used for betterment and spiritual growth—opportunities for healing moments. We don't realize that undesirable events might be steering us toward something even greater than we initially expected. This is especially true with failed relationships, careers, or relocations. Rather than clinging to a lifeless tree, we could let go and find better shade.

♥

Sometimes it feels like things are working against us, when in reality, our lives are being engineered for better things to come.

You can exercise control in two ways—holding on or letting go. One will cause you to suffer, and the other is momentarily uncomfortable but ultimately will give you peace.

Sometimes it feels like things are working against us, but in reality, they are engineering our lives for much better things to come.

I recently met a gentleman who was forced to move out of his residence of thirty years. Our discussion made it clear that all sense of control had been taken away from him. Once he shifted his power from resisting the change to the possibility of better things to come, he felt relieved. He realized he would make a good profit on his home and make new friends elsewhere. Besides, most of his friends had already moved or passed away, and he didn't feel close to the current residents. In the end, he'd gain a pocketful of unexpected income, a new location of his choice, and the possibility of satisfying friendships.

♥

Suffering is optional.

When bad things happen, it's only natural to feel powerless. A lack of control can be painful. But when we don't let go, our pain turns into suffering. Suffering is optional. I've often clung to beehives that caused me to get stung again and again. Tremendous relief came when I finally let go and backed far away.

I hung on to relationships that were dead or deadly, each time sucking away at my self-esteem. Instead of letting go and focusing on more important things like my children, I wasted precious moments on impossible scenarios with friends, lovers, and sometimes even patients who were not willing to grow in healthy ways. I couldn't see that I was unconsciously drawn to people who had the same brokenness as some of my childhood caretakers. I didn't realize that I would have to be the one to take care of my own brokenness and stop trying to fix someone else—especially when they had no interest in change. It took time to learn that the best way to heal my inner child was to be a good parent to myself and my own children, a good friend, and a helper to people who wanted to change. The more I worked on myself, the better person I was to others.

♥

> Seen through the lens of love, you'll be able to
> perceive that all things are working for your
> highest good, always.

Perception vs. Reality

There's no such thing as losing control over anything but yourself. You always have the power to see any situation as a success or a failure. Seen through the lens of love, you'll be able to perceive that all things are working for your highest good, always. What if you changed your perception of victimhood and replaced it with victory-hood? You might just find you'd eliminated most of the discomfort that comes with change. That's what the voice of love wants for you. When an undesirable event occurs, you'll perceive this as a gift instead of a curse. You'll embrace the pain and allow it to free you from an unworkable situation. Just because you tilled the garden doesn't mean it will grow. You don't throw down your rake and walk away. What if you planted the bush beans in the wrong location, in a spot that doesn't get enough sun? What if the soil didn't have enough nitrogen for the corn you were trying to grow? These are only failures in the outcome. They are gains in experience and knowledge. You take what you've learned, apply the new knowledge, and do even better each time you plant. You continue to pull out the weeds that choke out new growth and rob the garden of its nutrients. Eventually, you'll have a garden beyond your wildest dreams.

♥

Healthy partners challenge one another, consequently helping to lift any chains that bind the other to failure.

When we give our power to external forces, we don't realize that we're exercising the wrong control. For example, sitting back and expecting God (or someone else) to fix everything is magical thinking. Success is a collaboration with the unseen. Believing God is punishing us for wrongdoing or that our spouse, boss, family, or friend is preventing success is a way to avoid responsibility. Healthy partners challenge one another, consequently helping to lift any chains that bind the other to failure.

Take one of my patients, for example. Sarah was unhappily married, but she'd given her power and control to her husband, Fred. Though successful and a good provider, he was rarely home. He worked long hours, served on several boards, and golfed all weekend. When he was home, he constantly found fault with her and the "messy" house. He'd drink every night, becoming even more withdrawn from conversation or contact. The marriage had been stagnant for years.

Sarah felt that no matter how much she did for Fred, she could never measure up to his expectations. Over the years, she lost her sense of self.

She had lost all interest in the things she loved—going to art galleries, swimming, and traveling. She knew things could be better, but she listened to the inner voice that told her, *Don't rock the boat. You don't want to wind up in a divorce.*

Sarah silently suffered and felt like her life had no meaning or purpose. She wanted to break free from her internal prison, but she'd become afraid of the world "out there." For the past twenty years, her life had rotated around her family and home. When she thought of separating . from Fred, fearful thoughts flooded her mind. *You can't be all alone. How are you supposed to live? Will your kids hate you for getting a divorce? You will have to start a whole new life, without a job or a support system.* These fears immobilized her. She didn't realize that they were keeping her entwined in a whirlwind of denial and self-doubt.

Sarah's fear had locked her into two thoughts. First, if she exercised control over her life, she'd wind up divorced, and second, she would have to face a world that she wasn't equipped to handle.

Finally, one day I asked her, "Why are you on this planet?"

Sarah looked at me like a deer in the headlights. Several minutes went by, and then she said she had no idea. Her parents had always told her what to do, and currently she assigned all power over to her husband. She had no identity of her own.

I then said, "Is there some reason you can't have both—a marriage and a career?"

Once that thought took hold, Sarah felt a stirring sense of excitement and possibility. She realized she'd been under the control of her husband just like she'd been with her parents in childhood. Nothing had changed. Her assignment was to think about what she'd like to be when she was all grown up. She laughed until she cried. She could not believe she'd spent so much of her life bound by hidden fears.

During the next session, Sarah reported she'd always loved art and had dreamed of working in an art museum. But she'd never had a formal education. Her parents had never supported her college dreams. They thought she should marry Mr. Right and live happily ever after. Sarah was terrified of going back to school and didn't know how to begin. When we did a Google search for college for older, nontraditional students, we found all kinds of opportunities and resources. She decided to take the leap and make a few calls.

When Sarah told Fred she wanted to get a college degree, he smiled but looked skeptical. It took a while for Fred to wrap his mind around the new Sarah, but once she was engaged and full of enthusiasm, he enjoyed having the woman with whom he'd fallen in love back. Sarah finished her first semester with honors. She then secured a part-time job in her local museum doing menial work. She framed her first paycheck and put it above her vanity. "It always reminds me that I am in charge of my life, and I will never again be the victim of my fears," she told me.

Like Sarah, many of us have distorted our lives by misusing power and control, either by giving others power over us or attempting to control them. In either case, we make our happiness dependent on what other people are doing. By not facing our fears, we cause our relationships to become dull and lifeless. We aren't supposed to sacrifice our own identity and life's purpose for the sake of artificial safety (i.e., another person or a role we define in context of another person). That's not why we're here.

♥

We aren't supposed to sacrifice our own identity and life's purpose for the sake of artificial safety.

The Downside of Force

Forcing our way through life into the things *we* desire is the opposite of being controlled. You will do whatever it takes, right or wrong, to make something happen. But force has two negative consequences. First, you might step on too many toes, hurt someone, and be in a position where they're eventually trying to get even with you. At the very least, when you hurt someone, you battle your conscience for the rest of your life. Plus, when you force an outcome, you'll never know if someone did something out of love or out of fear. The latter never feels good.

The second negative consequence of exerting force is less visible but even more costly. Had you not exerted your will to make something happen, you may have been on a perfect path to success, but you'll never know where that natural path would have led you. You can be assured it would have been much smoother with a better result had you done the footwork and allowed the outcome to organize itself into fruition. It's the same principle as planting a seed and waiting. You can't tug on the tender shoots to hasten their growth. You do your part and wait for nature to do the rest.

♥

. . . learn how to be uncomfortable with the unknown.

Relinquishing control means becoming an observer of your own emotions and not letting them overly steer your beliefs about yourself and others or your behaviors. You learn how to be uncomfortable with the unknown. You know when to wait and when to follow through and act.

Maybe you're familiar with the game follow-the-dots. There's a series of numbered dots on a piece of paper, and when you connect the dots from one number to the next, an image appears. The picture isn't clear from just staring at the dots; you have to take a pen or pencil and connect them. The paths of our lives operate the same way. We must do the preparations ourselves, but success is a collaboration. We need to wait for the next sign on our life map to appear for the dots to connect so that the miracles can happen.

Sometimes it seems like things will never happen, but in these periods of unknowing, we develop spiritual muscle. It's the same principle as working out. At first, you don't see a change when you begin to eat healthily and exercise. You probably won't see a difference for quite a while, but things are subtly changing every day. A few months later, when you look at an old photo, you can see how much progress you've made. The change was happening all along. It just didn't seem like it. The same is true when we grow spiritually—it's subtle but profound.

♥

Sometimes it seems like things will never happen, but in these periods of unknowing, we develop spiritual muscle.

The less we exert force, the more we see the plan unfold, and it is far more remarkable than we envisioned. Even more fascinating, the dots often appear from totally unexpected sources.

Every job from which I was ever fired led to something better. When I was let go from my waitressing job at age eighteen, a neighbor offered me a position working for the county department of adult education. When that job ended, a law firm hired me. When I was let go from that job, a better one came along at a more prestigious law firm. That one didn't work out either. Job insecurity made me realize I needed a college degree to become independent. As a high school dropout with a GED, I didn't feel smart enough to go to college. This was reinforced by my low SAT scores and my new college advisor telling me to go for an easier degree than psychology. Still, there was a loving voice inside of me that said, *Don't pay attention to any of that. Just enroll. You can do this.* I thanked the advisor for his guidance and then asked him to enroll me in the psychology department.

I was utterly amazed when I graduated with honors from the two-year program in a year and a half—next, a bachelor's degree, and then, a master's degree. I was fulfilling my dream to become a psychotherapist.

While I was in supervision for psychotherapy licensure, my mentor told me to go for a doctorate in adult education. I told him that was impossible. I was divorced with two children, working full-time in private practice. While I was giving him all the excuses, he picked up the phone and made an appointment with the department head to set up an interview. You're probably wondering why I'm talking about not trying to control others, and I just gave an example of someone who exercised control in my life. Here's the difference. He wasn't trying to control me; he saw something in me I couldn't fathom, and he empowered me. Had I not followed through, he would have understood. He didn't have a hidden agenda, and my decision didn't affect him, but it certainly brought me full circle.

I'd been a graduate of an adult education program, and I'd worked for the department of adult education. And several years after my supervisor placed that call, I earned a doctorate in adult education.

For my dissertation, I developed an addictions training program for the continuing education program at Palm Beach Community College, the same place I'd obtained my first college degree. My career path has led me from a graduate of adult education to a doctorate in adult education. All the messes I'd made from quitting high school and getting married too soon had turned into miracles, and all the dots connected.

♥

While the voice of love is always there to help us take control of any situation, help isn't available unless you direct your energy for change back to yourself.

You don't have control over anyone or anything outside of you. You have a choice. You can cling to unworkable situations or imagine you are swinging from one star to the next, letting go for bigger and brighter things to come. While the voice of love is always there to help us take control of any situation, help isn't available unless you direct your energy for change back to yourself. You are the master of your universe, but you need help from the universe to master yourself.

The most important person you will ever control is yourself. I'm talking about claiming so much personal empowerment that you know you are the manager of your life. It worked for me. It worked for Sarah. And it will work for you once you've tapped into the part of your mind that gives you that power (your belief in your ability) and you rule from the part of your mind that wants to keep you out of prison.

♥

You are the master of your universe, but you need help from the universe to master yourself.

But how do you take back control over yourself?

First, you accept the fact that you are wasting your precious energy trying to control anyone or anything but yourself. This doesn't mean you quit. You simply let go. Quitting is final. Letting go is the freedom to venture into the unknown, which might include revisiting past situations over time because they have evolved into a better fit. For example, you're more prepared for a particular career, one or both partners have matured and are more compatible, your desire to relocate is now open, and you're ready to take risks. Sometimes, you just know when the time is right or not.

♥

Quitting is final. Letting go is the freedom to venture into the unknown . . .

Then you decide that you will honestly face the voice of fear that's driving you. You fire the voice of fear as your manager and replace it with the voice of love so that you can have your healing moment. Once you do this, you have opened the door to freedom. The shadows have been exposed, and you are free to walk through them like the invisible clouds they are.

Marsha was obsessing over whether her husband was fooling around on her. He reminded her of other men who'd betrayed her trust. One day while searching through his drawer, looking for a hotel receipt or some other type of evidence of infidelity, she realized she was acting crazy. She asked the voice of love to help her. It said, *This is not why you're here. This is about your past. You have more important things to do than violate your husband's privacy and trust.* Once she recovered from the shock of such a direct message, she felt a surge of relief. From that point forward, Marsha redirected herself to healing her past and remaining in the now instead of focusing on what her husband might be doing wrong.

By facing the fear that's driving you and replacing it with a genuine love for yourself and others, you'll be able to let go of your self-defeating patterns and focus on personal growth.

♥

By facing the fear that's driving you and replacing it with a genuine love for yourself and others, you'll be able to let go of your self-defeating patterns and focus on personal growth.

When you find yourself immobilized by someone else's control or find yourself trying to change others, harness that energy back to personal change. Power struggles are like tug of wars, and if you let go of the rope, change happens. You can train yourself to first listen to your fearful thoughts and then replace them with decisions based on love. And if you can't immediately create the win-win scenario you want, hang in there. You may have dodged a potential disaster, or perhaps it simply wasn't meant to be because there's something better waiting for you just down the road. All you need to do is connect the dots as they are revealed to you. Think of yourself as a rolling stone, smoothing away edges and going gently down the stream.

The more you turn your efforts inward, the more control you will have, and that's where the miracles happen.

♥

**The more you turn your efforts inward,
the more control you will have, and that's where the
miracles happen.**

Your Healing Moment Exercise 2:
How to Use Control to Master Yourself

These exercises will help you to refocus control on yourself. Once that happens, everything else will change along with you.

1. When you were young, did you feel you were under too much control? Not enough?

   _____

   _____

   _____

2. Do you believe that there are certain things you have control of and other things over which you have no control?

   _____

   _____

   _____

3. What are some of the times you allowed yourself to be controlled by others?

   _____

   _____

   _____

4. When have you attempted to exert control over others?

_____

_____

5. What do you want?
   a. Personally?

   _____

   _____

   b. Professionally?

   _____

   _____

   c. For others?

   _____

   _____

6. What is the plan to achieve these goals? What part is yours? What part belongs to someone else?

_____

_____

_____

7. Are you committed to doing your part without trying to control the other factors?

_____

_____

_____

Three-Step Exercise for Control

1. Write down a situation that you want to control.
2. Write down your fear(s) if your desired outcome fails. (For example, "If I lose this friend, I won't have anyone to do things with." "If I don't get this job, I won't be able to pay my bills." "If we break up, I'll never be able to feel this way about anyone again.")
3. Now, ask the voice of love to help you let go of the fear of lack and trust the unknown. Ask for a sense of direction. Be willing to follow that intuitive guidance.

Chapter 3

THIRD PATH: TRUST

You Are the Most Important Person You Will Ever Trust

Nothing outside yourself can save you; nothing outside
yourself can give you peace.
—*A Course in Miracles (Lesson 70)*

Here's the thing about trust: if you don't ever risk trusting, you'll never learn to trust yourself. Trust means that you have confidence that what you expect to happen will happen. And if it doesn't happen, you can trust that you will be all right. Trust and feeling safe go hand in hand.

The First People We Trust (or Not) Are Our Parents

The first trusting relationship is with our caretakers. In a healthy situation, babies learn to trust that their needs will be met, including safety. It should be guaranteed that someone will feed, clothe, cuddle, and protect the infant. The care may not be perfect, but it's good enough to build a steady sense of assurance, leading to a secure attachment with the caretaker. This sense of security carries over into the child's perception of life and the world. When these basic needs aren't met, children learn they can't trust what will happen.

As youngsters, we rely on people because we must in order to survive. Some are trustworthy; some are not. When someone lets us down, we lose trust and no longer feel safe with that person or situation. When children are physically or verbally abused, they learn that people are here to hurt

33

them rather than to love them. When a parent sexually abuses a child, the child feels like an object instead of a human being with boundaries and respect. When a child is put in an adult role too young, they learn to take care of others (codependency) rather than to have a balance of healthy give-and-take. When children are neglected, they don't feel worthy or valuable.

Another form of distrust occurs when children are betrayed. If a child is promised something and then—without explanation—it doesn't happen, the child learns they can't trust what people tell them. Some caretakers even go so far as to gaslight their kids and tell them they never made the promise in the first place. This causes children to question their own perception of reality.

We might form a wall to protect ourselves from being vulnerable when hurt or betrayed. Eventually, that wall becomes the voice of fear that won't let love in. Do you want to go through life standing on the outside, watching everyone else on the playground of life?

One patient of mine, Chris, had been severely abused by her father. She was frequently slapped and shoved around. She was told she was stupid and wouldn't amount to anything. Her healing moment came when she had her first child. She recognized something was seriously wrong when she couldn't feel maternal love and instead felt angry. In therapy, as she unpeeled the layers of her past, she understood that she'd never formed a secure connection with a safe and loving parent, and she must learn how to do that now. As she began to accept her past and grieve the pain she'd kept inside, her heart began to gently open to the voice of love. The more she grew to love herself, the more she was able to love her baby and break the family abuse pattern.

Constantly protecting yourself against ever being hurt or tricked does not provide a guarantee of safety. Insulating oneself under the fear of being betrayed is like living in a box with peepholes, watching the world behind paper walls. You may not get hurt, but you live in the dark—a life closed off from forgiveness—by keeping love out.

It is far better to go through life as a hurt, loving fool than a shrewd, unloved fool. Just like physical injuries, all emotional wounds heal over time. If used correctly, we learn from the pain how to be more giving and love better, and relationships become more fulfilling. But the person who harbors pain and won't risk being hurt again has a heart that shrivels and dies.

♥

It is far better to go through life as a hurt, loving fool than a shrewd, unloved fool.

Guided by the voice of love, it is possible to feel safe and trust no matter what has happened. Of course, this doesn't mean bad things will never happen. But you will know how to provide the right kind of protection for yourself, and it won't be based on fear. You can become like a rock that loses its jagged edges as it tumbles down a stream. The journey only gets smoother along the way. Your heart gets stronger, better able to love.

♥

Guided by the voice of love, it is possible to feel safe and trust no matter what has happened.

We've been conditioned to believe that we are at the whim of external events and forces and have nothing to do with the cause of those happenings. Nothing could be further from the truth.

Trusting Yourself

As the masters of our own universes, as we established in the last chapter, we're responsible for our peace of mind, and we can learn how to attain that state of mind no matter what goes on around us. Even people who've suffered unimaginable betrayals at the hands of their caretakers can heal and use those experiences to help others. They can decide to heal their pain and live in the present moment with loving consciousness.

When unforeseen misfortunes fall upon us as adults, we still have control over how we react to those situations. We can embrace the harsh winds of life or, like Don Quixote, fight the windmills. Every misfortune presents two differing paths: a gateway to living in fear or an opportunity for emotional, spiritual, and even financial growth. The bigger the mess, the greater the miracle.

♥

> Every misfortune presents two differing paths:
> a gateway to living in fear or an opportunity for
> emotional, spiritual, and even financial growth.

Aside from childhood trauma, most of what happens to us is our own creation. Have you trusted or ignored your internal warnings? How many times have you said, "I knew that would happen; I should have listened to my gut."? One voice was cautioning you, but the voice of fear was louder than the warning. Has a fear of losing an opportunity or disappointing someone or concerns about others' opinions of you ever overridden your internal voice of love? You wanted something—a relationship with a person rife with red flags, a high-paying job that carried hellacious hours, a second mortgage on your house to pay for an addition that seemed like a good idea at the time—and the voice of fear convinced you to silence your concerns rather than take steps to protect yourself. Then, after you got burned, you failed to realize it was you who stuck your hand in the fire in the first place. We have inner guidance, but we must learn to place that guidance at the center of all trust.

When we listen to the voice of love, we can reduce risks by establishing clear and indisputable agreements and boundaries that produce win-win instead of win-lose outcomes. Sometimes the outcome might mean walking away because the inner voice has warned us to do so. It's better to feel short-term disappointment than experience consequences that take years to recover from. Some people are reckless about whom they trust, and others don't trust anyone, not even themselves. Your inner voice is the most important voice you'll ever trust. If you can cultivate your belief in its guidance, you will gain the control over the decision-making that you seek.

♥

It's better to feel short-term disappointment than experience consequences that take years to recover from.

One patient, Bob, was offered an investment deal by Randy, whom he'd recently met at a chamber of commerce meeting. If Bob invested $50,000 in the company, he'd receive stock and the opportunity to earn an excellent return on his investment, plus free airline travel for the rest of his life. Bob felt uneasy, but since he knew some of the other investors, and he hadn't learned to trust the voice of love, he dismissed his queasiness and wrote the check. Unfortunately, his decision to be ruled by his impulses rather than his inner warnings was an expensive learning experience.

During the next few months, whenever Bob asked Randy what was happening, he received nothing but the runaround of non-answers again and again. When Bob finally confronted Randy about his partner's lack of accountability, he received an email. "Oh, sorry," it read. "I thought I told you. I had to fold the company, too much competition."

Bob wasn't surprised, but he was angry with himself for making such an avoidable mistake. He'd invested a good portion of his savings, and now he would never receive a return on his money. He'd simply written a check to a con man, who never held a scintilla of accountability. Bob felt like a fool and could only turn his rage on himself. Not only did he lose money, but he also lost confidence in his ability to make good decisions.

If Bob had paid attention to the uneasiness he'd felt, he could have avoided the financial loss. But, instead, he listened to the other part of his mind that told him to ignore those feelings and make the investment.

His fear of missing out on a potentially lucrative investment overrode his internal warning. Had he chosen to act from love instead of fear, he could have kept his money for a better investment down the road. Instead, he had to bear the loss, suffer embarrassment, and wrestle with diminished self-esteem.

Like Bob learned, and like you may have learned in your own life (I know I have), some of the worst betrayals are self-inflicted. We choose to do something even though we sense it's wrong. We don't heed the warnings, and then we suffer the consequences. This could result in living with guilt or causing preventable harm to ourselves or others.

For years, whenever the voice of love told me to wait, I didn't. I was impulsive and didn't take the time to let things play out. I'd take the wrong offer or the inappropriate relationship or agree to do something that wasn't right for me. Oh, I heard the voice all right—"Maybe you ought to think about that before you decide"—but I'd swat the warning away like an unwanted fly. Fortunately, those many mistakes have given me the incentive to now have an iron-clad commitment to the voice of love.

Most recently, I was searching for an assisted living facility for my mom. It was an intense process and involved a lot of interviews and information processing. The second facility seemed perfect, and I was ready to commit, but the warning came: "Maybe you should interview all of the facilities before you decide?" Sure enough, the last facility turned out to be the prettiest, the closest, and the least expensive. It also offered the most services. Unlike the others, it provided me the opportunity to see my mom every day.

--------------------------------------- ♥ ---------------------------------------

Without learning to *trust* the inner voice of love,
I would have allowed negative emotions to consume me

Then later, under new management, everything changed for the worse, and I had to move my mom again. My ego wanted to retaliate, but

I had to channel that anger and fear into constructive action as my mom's advocate. Without learning to *trust* the inner voice of love, I would have allowed negative emotions to consume me and wouldn't have been able to look out for my mom's best interests. Life is constantly changing, and we can either reject it or embrace it.

Trusting the Voice of Love to Help Others

Trust isn't always about self-protection. It's also about helping others. One of my friends was doing volunteer work tutoring underprivileged elementary children. One day her student asked if she had anything to eat. The school's breakfast program had shut down, leaving many young children hungry. My friend was shocked that the young girl was hungry and turned her distraught feelings into action. She organized a food drive in her neighborhood, resulting in the delivery of truckloads of food to the school. Then later, she started a clothing and school supply donation drive, all still in effect years later. She could have handed her student a snack, but instead, she listened to the voice of love and created a food and essential needs program for the entire school. Her student got a full tummy, and my friend felt gratification that would last her forever. We are constantly presented with opportunities to help people; we need only to watch and listen for those chances to share the love.

♥

We are constantly presented with opportunities to
help people; we need only to watch and listen for those
chances to share the love.

Reckless Distrust

Some people have the opposite problem: reckless distrust. They remain frozen by indecision and won't make any decisions at all. The core fear here is a lack of trust in anyone or anything, including themselves. They are disconnected from their internal compass. As a result, opportunities pass by them like crates full of gold just waiting to be delivered to their doorstep. When no one answers the door, the gold is returned to its source.

These people are often afraid to take risks. And people who are afraid to take risks are often operating under the belief that it's not all right to make mistakes and that failure is unacceptable. They're the opposite of the reckless risk-taker: when an opportunity presents itself, they obsess over every detail, and while they are scrutinizing the minutia, the deal passes them by.

Indecisiveness is one form of fear that keeps us in a state of twisted conflict. Opportunities are missed: the ideal romantic partner, a shot at financial gain, the perfect career can all slip through our fingers. How often have you heard someone say, "I should have married that person," "I should've never moved," "If I would have made that investment, I'd be a millionaire now," or "I wish I'd taken that job. Instead, I'm stuck with half the pay and none of the benefits the other position offered."

♥

Indecisiveness is one form of fear that keeps us in a state of twisted conflict.

For example, more than anything, James wanted to live in an area of town that he couldn't afford. His mission was to save enough money to buy his dream home in that neighborhood someday. Then, one day, out of thin air, a real estate broker approached him about buying his current house.

This broker had a buyer who would pay James more than his home's market value because it was in the school district where he wanted to raise his kids. At first, James was excited. If he accepted the offer, he'd net enough that, when combined with his savings, he'd be able to move to his dream neighborhood. But then fear gripped him. "What if I miss my current house?" he thought. "What if I lose my job, and I can't afford the new house?"

James spoke with his family and friends. Even though they all were supportive, he couldn't get unstuck from the fear that gripped him. Weeks went by while James continued to crunch numbers and ruminate over whether to go forward. Eventually, the broker called him and said that his client couldn't wait any longer and had bought a different house.

♥

> *. . . when we recognize how we block ourselves and change our fearful perceptions, new opportunities present themselves.*

Fear of failure stopped James from fulfilling his wish. He was afraid of making a mistake. Because of his failure to trust himself and act, he lost the invitation to capitalize on his dream. Fortunately for James, he learned from his mistake, and when we recognize how we block ourselves and change our fearful perceptions, new opportunities present themselves. Years later, when he had the chance to sell his house and buy in his dream neighborhood, he didn't let it pass him by. Instead, he bypassed his fear, listened to his internal guidance, and sought advice about things he didn't understand. After speaking with several experts to evaluate the cost, benefits, and expenses of the home, he was able to feel secure in his decision to move forward.

When we don't trust that inner voice of love, we set ourselves up for failure. Sometimes it's financial, and sometimes it's romantic. Sometimes it leads to consequences we can recover from, like James experienced, especially when we have the courage to change our mindset from fear to love.

Nancy's dream was to get married and start a family. For several years, she'd been dating Jack, an attorney, and even though she suspected his infidelities, she dismissed her feelings and remained loyal to him. During their courtship, she'd met two different men at work who showed an interest in her and who were ready for marriage and kids. But out of loyalty to Jack, she wouldn't give them the time of day. She'd also turned down a work scholarship for college because Jack thought it would take up too much of her time. As life slipped by, Nancy found herself in the same place as she had been eight years earlier—no marriage, no kids, no closer to her dream. Even though Nancy wasn't happy, she dismissed the loving voice that told her she deserved better and to move on.

Nancy was devastated when Jack broke up with her to be with someone else. She became furious when she heard a few months later that Jack was engaged. It was only then that it hit her: Jack was never in love with her. She'd acted out her fantasy as a willing participant, and now she didn't have a marriage or kids, but Jack would have both. Nancy was grief-stricken and embarrassed that she'd allowed herself to be used and had pretended Jack loved her despite his actions otherwise.

Fortunately for Nancy, her healing moment came when she realized she'd abandoned herself in the relationship with a man and vowed never to do so again. Her miracle was to forgive both Jack and herself. She embraced a new attitude—that of someone who had dreams to fulfill and a life of her own. She enrolled in college and focused on a new career. She turned her mess into the miracle of trusting herself, instead of being someone who turned her life over to someone else's best interests. Once she started working in banking, she met someone whom she began to date. He fell madly in love with her. It didn't take long for him to decide he wanted a life with Nancy, and they were married a year later.

Can you identify with either of these examples? If so, it's probably not your fault that you haven't learned to trust yourself. Most people haven't been encouraged to listen to their inner voice. Children are finely tuned in to what feels right and wrong, but if they aren't taught to cultivate a trusting relationship with their internal guidance system, the connection fades out. When parents invalidate a child's (accurate) perception, the child learns to distrust what they perceive, even when it's 100 percent correct.

If you haven't learned to trust your inner voice, though, you can start now. After all, it's never too late to learn how.

Making mistakes is a part of learning to trust. There's nothing wrong with making mistakes, even if we make the same mistakes again and again—as long as we're learning and growing from those experiences. That's the key to actual change. But to find the path to self-trust as adults, we need to look further back, to how we did or did not receive a foundation of trust when we were young.

♥

If you haven't learned to trust your inner voice, you can start now. After all, it's never too late to learn how.

Our First Relationships Teach Us about Trust

When we were born, we didn't arrive with a playbook for life, nor were our parents handed a parenting manual. Parenting is the most crucial task ever bestowed upon anyone, yet most of what we learn is intergenerationally passed down from caretakers, educational systems, and religion. As essential as they are, most of these resources are limited. Parents do what they were taught as kids, and as I have said, parents can make mistakes. The education system isn't fully equipped to teach many life skills, such as problem-solving and conflict resolution. And religion doesn't always teach children how to use their minds for the best decision-making purposes.

A child can be taught right from wrong, but rules mean little until those concepts are tested and internalized. For example, if a child is taught to be honest and then cheats on a test or steals from their parent's wallet, they suffer a sense of wrongdoing. This uncomfortable feeling is the natural consequence of an unwise decision. If caught and treated punitively, the child learns to be afraid of telling the truth. Children are quite capable of learning from their mistakes and most likely will do so if they are taught self-evaluation and correction.

Raining negativity on a child's head or punishing them for typical childhood errors doesn't produce better human beings. On the contrary, it fosters children with low self-esteem, who are more likely than not to make more mistakes, not fewer.

If a child is taught how to trust their inner voice and follow its guidance, they will be less inclined to test the limits. Likewise, when a child makes a mistake, if the parent lovingly holds the child accountable, the child understands why the act they did was wrong and will be forever empowered.

Consider this exchange as an example:

"Johnny, do you know why you stole Bobby's toy?"
"No. I just wanted it."
"So, you just did what you wanted to do? Did you know it was wrong to steal Bobby's toy?"
Johnny might nod affirmatively.
"How did you know it was wrong?"
"I know it's wrong. I just did it."
"So, something told you it was wrong, but you didn't listen?"
Johnny will probably nod yes again.
"Do you feel good about doing the wrong thing?"
"No."
"Can you tell me why it's not a good choice to take someone else's things?"
"Because it's not mine, and it's not fair for me to take it."
"Johnny, it's okay to make mistakes, but what are you going to do about it?
"Give it back."
"Do you think you should apologize?"
"Yeah."

This type of dialogue does several things. First, the child is taught that it's okay to make mistakes but also that mistakes must be corrected. It eliminates anger and punishment and cultivates the child's connection with an inner voice, a place where a basic sense of self-value and the value of others can be discerned. Second, the parent is empowering the child to understand the two voices of love and fear. Third, rather than enabling the wrong behavior, the parent holds the child accountable to take responsibility and apologize for their mistake so that it doesn't turn into long-term guilt, or resentment on the part of the child's friend. Finally, the child is given all the power they will ever need to be a good friend; a successful student; mindful of others; and an upstanding, righteous, and spiritually self-directed person. Children raised this way will follow the laws of the land but will never be anyone's robot.

It's such a simple practice—discourse over punishment—yet it's so rarely utilized.

♥

It's okay to make mistakes and learn to trust yourself at the same time.

Many of us weren't taught to stay connected to our own inner guidance, but that doesn't mean we can't learn now. You can re-parent yourself at any time. The voice of love is always with you. It's okay to make mistakes and learn to trust yourself at the same time. Those mistakes can help you realize that you are better off listening to the voice that wants you to succeed, not the one that sets you up for failure.

No matter how big a mess your mistakes have made, you can turn all of them into miracles. If you learn and grow from those experiences, you can become wiser and more gifted. Many people achieved fame by overcoming their mistakes before making considerable contributions to humanity. Michael Jordan couldn't make the high school varsity team because he was too short, but he persisted until he was tall enough and had developed enough skill to become one of the greatest basketball players of all time.[1] Oprah Winfrey suffered abuse early in her career but learned to turn those experiences into strength and become a "real woman."[2] Steve Jobs never had a relationship with his biological father and was ousted by his own company for his difficult personality but learned from his mistakes and returned to make Apple hugely successful.[3] Thomas Edison was deaf in one ear, started his career selling candy and newspapers on trains, was branded as someone who couldn't keep a job,[4] and became one of the greatest inventors of all time.[5] The all-star tennis pro Serena Williams, who's had her share of setbacks, says, "I really think a champion is defined not by their wins but by how they can recover when they fall."[6] Walt Disney, raised with an abusive father, endured multiple business failures,[7] was turned down over three hundred times by bankers and financiers, and still managed to break through these barriers to achieve his pioneer role of success in film and theme parks.[8] They, like so many other icons, were driven by an inner force they learned to trust. All of these people fanned the fire of their gifts, not their failures. They refused to let failure deter them and even used their handicaps and setbacks as stepping-stones to success. They trusted their inner guidance. As a result, all these people turned messes into miracles, and you can do the same.

You are the most important person you will ever trust.

If you didn't learn to trust when you were young, you can teach yourself now. You must be willing to listen to the voice of love; it will never fail to give you the correct guidance. All your experiences can be lily pads that you use to cross the deepest waters to your highest goals. Once you turn away from the fear-driven voice and align your actions with the right voice, you can develop a deep sense of trust in yourself. You will no longer be at the mercy of others to exploit you—not even yourself.

You are the most important person you will ever trust.

Your Healing Moment Exercise 3: Developing Self-Trust

You are the most important person you will ever trust to guide you. The following questions will help you to identify the roots of distrust and how you can learn to trust your inner voice regardless of the past.

1. Do you trust yourself and your decisions?

    _____

    _____

    _____

2. How did you develop that trust or distrust?

_____

_____

_____

3. List three decisions that you later regretted.

_____

_____

_____

4. Now write down the two opposing messages you received. What did the loving warning voice tell you? What did the other voice say?

_____

_____

_____

5. Do you have a vision that you haven't accomplished? Have you allowed failure to stop you?

_____

_____

_____

6. Now write down how you could turn one of those regretful situations into a miracle.

_____

_____

_____

7. How can you use all your past misfortunes as paths to a successful future?

_____

_____

_____

Three-Step Exercise for Trust

1. Write down something you are trying to achieve but haven't yet accomplished. Focus on your natural gifts.
2. Close your eyes, and ask the voice of love to help you.
3. Write down the information that you receive, and be willing to follow through.

Chapter 4

FOURTH PATH: FORGIVENESS

You Are the Most Important Person You Will Ever Forgive

Forgiveness is the key to happiness.
—*A Course in Miracles (Lesson 121)*

When we really live life—I mean stepping to the center of the stage instead of lurking in the stands—we're going to make mistakes. Some of them will be doozies. Some will hurt others. Sometimes, you will be the one who's hurt, deeply hurt. These experiences are part of the fiber of existence. Nature has its violent, aggressive side. Likewise, a life well-lived will also face the fires and floods of the human tempest. But stressful and even traumatic experiences can be used for growth. We can't always choose what happens in life, but we certainly can choose how we will react to challenging events and how long we will hold on to resentments or hurt feelings.

♥

**Resentment is the rust that corrodes
all loving relationships.**

Resentment is the rust that corrodes all loving relationships. Many people cannot forgive the mistakes they've made. Likewise, some people won't forgive the mistakes others have made. Every held resentment is like another heavy link added to a chain that binds you to your past.

Forgiveness is a process, though, and it always happens at the end of the grief cycle. We often think of grief as only arising in response to a loss, but any betrayal or harm that we experience or do to ourselves can also lead to grief, as that wrongdoing usually results in the loss of something: trust, respect, self-worth. We're rarely able to forgive if we haven't allowed ourselves to go through the stages of grief first. Elisabeth Kübler-Ross first wrote about the feelings and emotions that a person goes through when experiencing a loss: denial, anger, bargaining, and depression, all eventually leading to acceptance.[1]

---------------------------- ♥ ----------------------------

We're rarely able to forgive if we haven't allowed ourselves to go through the stages of grief first.

Other experts have developed their own theories, but most agree that in order to heal, emotions need to be experienced. And this doesn't mean intellectual healing; it means allowing yourself to feel the pain and get it out. I see many people do what I call spiritualizing (another word for sanitizing) their feelings. They use platitudes and slogans to cope with pain in place of grieving the pain. This only keeps everything bottled inside, and it's likely to create obsessive thoughts and depression. Only by experiencing your emotions can you find your way to acceptance.

There are two blocks that prevent forgiveness: anger and guilt. As mentioned earlier, both cover up fear, and we can't access the fear if we don't deal with the anger and guilt. If we don't go past these emotions, we can't access the third block to healing: pain.

Pain Is Normal; Suffering Is Optional

Learning how to release feelings in healthy ways starts in childhood. Many people have never learned to embrace their feelings, so they never reach forgiveness. There are reasons parents are ineffective at helping their children heal from pain. They tend to parent the way they were parented. If they cried, males were often told they were "sissies" in previous generations. This crazy intention was to turn a boy into a man. Mental toughness doesn't happen from shutting down emotions, it happens by overcoming them and choosing to forge through challenging situations. Even girls often disconnect emotionally. I remember hearing, "If you don't stop whining, I'll give you something to cry about." Parents told their children to be seen and not heard—as if they were little statues to merely sit upon a chair. If parents were abused, they tended to be abusive. Sometimes parents were exhausted from work and other responsibilities and didn't have the internal resources to be as present as they'd have liked.

Fortunately, in the past few decades, we've been provided more information on effective parenting. A child should be allowed to cry, and they should be held and cuddled when sad. Once the pain is out, the child can be restored to their natural state, free of grief. If a youngster is given the message that it's not okay to shed tears, they will learn to stuff their emotions down inside instead. Those tears can freeze into crystals that may never thaw.

♥

Nurturing the release of feelings applies to all emotions,
even the feelings we tend to classify as "negative."

Forgiveness Is Natural

If they're allowed to get out the negative feelings, kids won't harbor resentment. They get hurt, feel it, and express it, and when comforted, it's gone. I repeat, it's gone.

Nurturing the release of feelings applies to all emotions, even the feelings we tend to classify as "negative." For instance, if a child is angry, they should be taught to express anger effectively. Think in terms of talking it out versus acting it out. Instead of yelling or throwing something, a child can be taught to say how they feel without attack, such as "I'm angry because you won't let me go play with my friends." It's only natural to feel angry at times, like when you feel violated or something unfortunate has thwarted your plans. But people who can't manage their anger effectively tend to be aggressive (outrightly or passively) or violent. And they are likely to have significant problems in all their relationships. If you hold in anger, it can permeate other areas of your life (like any pollutant). But anger is an emotion that, once correctly vented, will subside. How do we do this? Some people write letters expressing their anger and never mail them. Others punch pillows or go to the gym and hit punching bags. One person I know chopped down dead trees to expel her anger. Others get relief from talking it out.

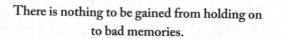

There is nothing to be gained from holding on to bad memories.

Unresolved anger turns into resentment. The smoldering embers in a fire burn away your freedom and joy. It's a heavy investment of precious wasted time. There is nothing to be gained from holding on to bad memories.

Tears Cleanse the Body and the Soul

There are two reasons for tears: cleaning the eyes and healing emotional pain. Any loss, no matter how big or small, is an emotional experience. If we don't face the pain of losing someone or something, we can remain stuck in denial, anger, and resentment—more bricks in the wall.

Just like anger, sorrow must be embraced. Saying goodbye and feeling the sadness is uncomfortable but restorative. Fighting back the tears will cause you to carry buckets of pain wherever you go. A good cry lets go of the pain and replaces it with peace and acceptance. And beyond acceptance is a final stage: meaning.

♥

A good cry lets go of the pain and replaces it with peace and acceptance.

David Kessler, the co-author of Kübler-Ross's book *On Grief & Grieving: Finding the Meaning of Grief Through the Five Stages of Grief,* added "finding meaning" as the sixth stage of grieving. Going beyond acceptance, when you can embrace the hidden gifts in a loss, you have completed the sixth phase.[2] Recognition of what you've gained in personal growth is the completion of this final stage. Being a better person, learning how to live alone, being more appreciative, finding a better job or life partner, using those experiences to help others, and growing spiritually are examples of finding meaning in loss.

One of my most heart breaking therapeutic relationships was with a woman named Melba, whose daughter had been senselessly murdered. The murderer had driven to meet his drug dealer, but instead of handing over the drugs, the dealer took the money and then ripped the gold chains off his customer's neck. Deranged with rage and long-term drug usage, the victim went home, got his rifle, returned to the scene of the crime, and started randomly shooting at innocent bystanders, including Melba's daughter.

Melba, like so many other people, was afraid to feel her pain. "If I open this door, I may never stop crying," she told me. The fear of losing control had cost her the loss of control. Holding in her pain prolonged her suffering—the very thing she most feared.

Melba was referred for therapy because it had been two years, and she could not get over her loss. Even though the murderer had been caught and charged with the crime, Melba couldn't sleep or concentrate. She sorely missed her daughter and couldn't stop thinking about the tragedy.

Once Melba took a leap of faith with me, her tragedy unraveled. It was apparent from the unemotional way Melba unpacked the tragedy that she was stuck in her pain. Perhaps it was the horror on my face as the facts of the event came out that unleashed the enormity of Melba's pain. Or maybe, once she opened the door, the emotions flooded out. She fluctuated between blaming herself and blaming the shooter.

She said, "I told my daughter to stay off that street corner. Bad things happen there. Why couldn't I get her to listen?"

She said, "Why was that boy allowed to come into my neighborhood, buy drugs, and then shoot people?"

She moaned in agony as she rocked and wailed for an entire hour.

The following session, Melba reported it was the best she'd felt in a long time. "A huge burden lifted off my heart," she declared. "I can breathe."

She'd held in her pain because her pastor told her it was necessary to forgive the sinner who murdered her daughter. This is a mistake often made by religious and spiritual advisors who don't recognize the need to grieve and prematurely speak of forgiveness.

Melba had opened the door to her pain and let it out, but she wasn't finished yet. It wasn't until she met the perpetrator face-to-face that she had her healing moment. About three months into therapy, he and his attorney requested a meeting with her and the public prosecutor. In addition to agreeing to jail time, he was offering her a cash settlement. At first, she boiled with rage. "How dare you think money will make anything better," she bellowed at him. "My daughter is gone. I'll never see her again."

He merely hung his head and whispered, "I'm sorry."

During her next session with me, she cried some more. She told me she had thought about the meeting and decided to accept the offer—not because she wanted the money but because it was a token of accepting his request for forgiveness.

In the middle of a sentence, Melba became quiet. She then looked up at me and said she felt sorry for the man who'd killed her daughter. He'd have to live with this the rest of his life, and she wondered how he would do that. "I actually feel some type of sorrow for him," she said. "I don't know what. I can't explain it. I'll learn how to live without my baby, but he'll never be able to live with what he's done. No money, no jail time will change that."

In that instant, Melba suddenly had her healing moment.

The following session, she told me she'd spoken with her pastor and told him she wanted to do something to help other people who'd lost their children. She said he was receptive. Not only had Melba experienced grief and forgiveness, but she'd also now found meaning by using her tragedy to help others.

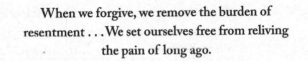

> When we forgive, we remove the burden of
> resentment . . . We set ourselves free from reliving
> the pain of long ago.

Resentment Punishes You Instead of Someone Else

When we forgive, we remove the burden of resentment, whether it's directed toward ourselves or others. We set ourselves free from reliving the pain of long ago.

Harboring resentment is a lot like carrying around a fifty-pound suitcase full of videos from every bad memory of your life. You constantly replay the films and relive the discomfort again and again, for no other purpose than self-torture. But that's only the tip of the iceberg.

At the root of every resentment is self-blame better known as guilt. Blaming others, and even ourselves, blocks the light of the spirit. All those barriers can dissolve instantly in the consciousness of love.

> Blaming others, and even ourselves,
> blocks the light of the spirit.

If you have a lasting grievance toward someone else, deep down you probably feel you did something wrong. You made a mistake—somehow, it's all your fault. Buried thoughts nag at you: *I should have listened to what other people told me; I was an idiot to trust that woman—she has a terrible reputation, but I thought I could help her.* Even abused children may ask, *What's wrong with me? What did I do to cause this abuse? How could I have been so stupid?*

We have all at some point done something we find difficult to live with. Sometimes these things feel so big that we get stuck inside them. Perhaps we regret the way we parented our kids. Or replay the time we stole something, betrayed a friend, or told a huge lie that hurt someone we loved. We're left with a lasting sense of shame and worthlessness. Even if amends have been made, the regret continues to be debilitating, stifling our dreams and aspirations. Without forgiveness, there's a feeling of rot that never leaves our core.

We've established that we have all made mistakes. Most of these are rooted in childhood reenactments of what we observed or how we were treated in our youth. Abusive behaviors are intergenerational and tend to be repeated. Most kids who have been programmed to lie, cheat, steal, or abuse, and who've not been held accountable for their own actions, will continue these behaviors as adults. Unless they see the light, these people will suffer in one form or another for their entire lives.

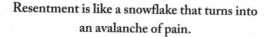

Resentment is like a snowflake that turns into an avalanche of pain.

Resentment is like a snowflake that turns into an avalanche of pain. The person you resent isn't the one suffering. You are. Letting go of resentment is like stepping out of that tumbling wave of ice and snow and finding the safe, pure security of the sunshine again.

It's Never Too Late to Apologize

Apologizing is a challenge. The shame of making mistakes and the fear of rejection makes it hard for people to say they're sorry. Pride can also be a barrier to atonement. It may be excruciating to admit what you did wrong and then offer to correct the mistake. But it's certainly better to come clean than to drag around suitcases full of garbage for the rest of your life.

---------------------------- ♥ ----------------------------

... the final step toward forgiving yourself is to
acknowledge the mistake and make amends.

In fact, the final step toward forgiving yourself is to acknowledge the mistake and make amends.

It takes a great deal of courage to face someone you've hurt, apologize to them, and then ask what you can do to make things better. Let's say the wrongdoing involved hurting someone through emotional betrayal or abuse. What might amends even look like? If appropriate, you could offer to pay for therapy, with or without your involvement. If the wrongdoing was monetary, offer to pay back the money. Often, acknowledging the error and offering a sincere apology is all it takes to soothe the wounds. If they refuse to accept your amends, consider donating to that person's favorite charity or do something nice for them or their family, anonymously.

You can't make someone forgive you. You can only extend the olive branch. But when you've made a heartfelt apology, you've done your part. In either case, you've released yourself from the burden of guilt and started the process of setting yourself free.

We know that some harms are greater and more complex than others. In cases where an apology could cause more harm than good, it's best to heal with a therapist, pastor, or some other confidant or professional. You wouldn't want to tell some unknowing person that you were sorry you'd had an affair with their loved one. Scrubbing one's conscience at the expense of harming others can cause a whole new set of conflicts and pain.

When Eddie first made amends to his parents for stealing their possessions and conning them for money, they were entirely skeptical. Eddie had been exploiting them ever since he started drinking and taking drugs in high school. They ultimately had to ban him from the house and change the locks on their doors.

Years later, when Eddie reappeared, he told his parents he was sober and wanted to make amends. He handed them a hundred dollars and said he would make regular payments until the debt was cleared for the damage he'd done.

Of course Eddie's parents didn't want to take the money or even associate with Eddie. He'd made promises before, and they'd given up on any expectations. This was the first time he had done something concrete, however. Out of love for their son, they accepted the money. Good thing they did. It was a symbol of forgiveness, allowing Eddie to work off his debt and earn back his self-esteem. Much to his parent's surprise, Eddie continued to make regular payments. With each payment, the fractured bond was repaired a bit more. The real miracle occurred years later when Eddie became so successful that he could move his parents into a house he had built just for them. Without healing and forgiveness, this could not have happened.

Guilt is fear's device to keep you stuck in the past. Brenda had her healing moment one morning when, as usual, she awakened with a jolt of anxiety when dreaming about her past mistakes. Finally, on the verge of a panic attack, she asked the voice of love for help and was told, "Going backward isn't helping anyone. If you want to be helpful to others, stop this." Over time, she began to share her past constructively only if it helped someone else. Otherwise, she stopped indulging in the game of self-deprecation.

No one needs to ask your forgiveness for you to forgive them. One of the cornerstones of my life was forgiving my mom. I was angry that she hadn't protected me from a raging alcoholic who emotionally devastated me at a tender age. She worked nights as a nurse, and I was angry that she had left me unattended for far too many hours and in a state bordering on psychosis. She never acknowledged the harm it caused me in my childhood even when I attempted to discuss it with her.

♥

No one needs to ask your forgiveness for you
to forgive them.

As an adult, I was resentful when she needed me. I kept my distance from her as I faced my own struggles. I saw her as another burden I didn't want to bear. But, as a single mom, I didn't mind using her for child-care. She was my biggest cheerleader with every accomplishment, but I was embarrassed when she'd publicly praise me. As much as I felt love from her, I couldn't feel close. When she moved far away to live with another relative, I remained ambivalent. This hardwired attitude remained through twenty-three years of my so-called recovery.

I knew I was mad about being raised with addiction. I had relatives with addiction. I blamed all that for my own addictions and failed marriages. When I became a psychotherapist, I vowed never to work with people suffering addiction. But, of course, that's precisely the type of referrals I received. (At the time I didn't know that almost every family is affected by addiction in some form.) I felt like there was a curse over my head for something I hadn't done.

If I'd checked my resentments and my guilt for not wanting a relationship with my mom, I would've enjoyed uninterrupted sobriety. Instead, it took a relapse for me to understand that I hadn't truly forgiven anyone, including myself. I never tied together that my issues with my mother were unhealed grievances until they were right in my face.

Now, not only physically sober but spiritually sober as well, I had a new approach. I'd heard my mom had lost her latest husband, and I wrote her a letter of condolence, expressing what a good man he had been. She promptly responded, and our healing began.

Over the next few years, we spent a lot of time together. My mom even stayed with me for months at a time. In the past, this would have driven me crazy. Now, I felt like I was getting to know her for the very first time. All my grievances melted into gratitude.

Those childhood experiences had given me the depth and breadth to help others. I could now see that every event in my life was part of the perfect design for my life's purpose: to help individuals and families who suffer addiction. Had I not experienced the effects of family addiction as well as my own, my effectiveness as a therapist would have been limited.

♥

> Holding yourself as unforgiveable is at the root
> of all resentment.

My mom was the cornerstone of my spirituality. With all the challenges, she planted the early seeds of my spirituality when she told me heaven or hell was right now. We choose which state we want to live in. She was the best nurse I'd ever witnessed, and she was my role model for providing competent care to others. She was not only highly skilled but kind. My mom didn't bake cookies or, for that matter, cook at all. She hated housework and didn't seem to care much about my grades. Yet, despite her flaws, she was my rock and never, ever said no when I needed her. These are some of the gifts she gave me, but my resentments had blocked the gratitude she deserved. Now, it is an honor and a privilege to be able to be of service to her when she can no longer care for herself.

Forgiveness gave me the best mom I could have ever had. Forgiveness was the miracle that turned our messy relationship into a loving one. It was the key that opened the forgiveness door of my mind and helped me realize what my addictions had done for me, not to me. Those struggles taught me more than I ever could have learned in the classroom, and they were the perfect curriculum to prepare me for my mission in life—to save lives from addiction. I was no longer a victim of addiction but a conduit to free others.

Forgiveness is like removing a cold, slimy blanket and exposing yourself to the sunlight for the first time. Holding yourself as unforgiveable is at the root of all resentment. What are you covering up with guilt? Will you let it go? When you do let go, you can be uplifted into the person you truly are.

———————————— ♥ ————————————

There is no mess so great that forgiveness won't transform it into a miracle.

We all have a birth certificate, but not a death certificate. Letting go of old pain means being able to enjoy the gift of life every new day.

You are the most important person you will ever forgive.

I invite you to join me. There is no mess so great that forgiveness won't transform it into a miracle.

———————————— ♥ ————————————

You are the most important person you will ever forgive.

Your Healing Moment Exercise 4: Finding Happiness through Forgiveness

Forgiveness blocks us from receiving the voice of love, the path to our inner light. This exercise is designed to help you turn pain and resentment into freedom and forgiveness.

1. Write down any resentments from which you have not recovered.

———————————————————————

———————————————————————

———————————————————————

2. Write a letter to that person or entity, expressing how you feel. Don't hold back on any thought or emotion. But remember, don't send the letter; instead, shred or burn it. If you still feel angry, pound pillows or go someplace safe and scream until there's nothing left but calmness. The purpose is to get the feelings out to free you from the negative emotions.

_____

_____

_____

3. What, if anything, are you blaming yourself for concerning these events?

_____

_____

_____

4. Write down something you feel guilty or ashamed of and wish you'd never done.

_____

_____

_____

5. Write yourself a letter stating why you can forgive yourself. For example, you made your choices based on the information you had at the time. You aren't supposed to know everything. You may not have been guided or taught to make better choices.

_____

_____

_____

6. Perhaps it was too painful to face the truth that led to an ultimate betrayal. It's okay to make mistakes, and it's okay to acknowledge them and then let go. Are you willing to allow these messes to transform into miracles? To whom would you apologize, and what would you say?

_____

_____

_____

7. When the time is right, be willing to have a healing conversation with the person who hurt you or vice versa. The intent of the encounter is to reach a level of compassion and understanding for the other, regardless of whether they feel the same toward you.

_____

_____

_____

Three-Step Exercise for Forgiveness

1. Go someplace where you feel comfortable and safe.
2. Review your thoughts toward anyone (including yourself) that you haven't forgiven.
3. Picture this relationship healed and loving. Allow yourself to feel the peace of a forgiven relationship.

Chapter 5

FIFTH PATH: RESPECT

No One Will Respect You More than Yourself

I am not the victim of the world I see.
—*A Course in Miracles (Lesson 31)*

Some people think that respect is an entitlement. While it's polite to be respectful to one another, the more a person demands respect, the less likely they will receive it. There's a big difference between being treated with respect and being respected. Someone being respectful because they are obligated is not genuine, heartfelt respect toward a person. The first comes from fear, and the latter stems from love.

If you're not being respected the way you'd like, it's time to understand why. You may be putting up with something because fear tells you to overlook how someone is acting toward you. In that case, you need to set boundaries, but remember, always with love. If you're certain your boundaries are reasonable and they are still ignored, you might be suffering a pseudo-relationship—one-sided.

The "We Program"

Life is a "we program." It's not a "me program" or a "you program." How you treat others and how people treat you reflects what you think of yourself. If you have self-respect, you treat others the way you'd like to be treated. Most of the time, that will be mirrored back to you.

---------------------------------♥---------------------------------

How you treat others and how people treat you
reflects what you think of yourself.

There are exceptions: aggressive, selfish, and mindless people. They can be intimidating and controlling and only interested in bullying their way through life. They should be avoided at all costs. But even aggressive people usually don't dominate the folks who have self-respect. When dealing with a bully, you must stand up for yourself.

Whether you're five or fifty-five, bullies don't pick on people who won't tolerate their abuse. Of course, anger should not be expressed through hitting or yelling. Adults with self-respect express their outrage after they've calmed down and can best state their case.

People feel each other out and know how far they can push someone. Once a comfort level is reached, there is an unconscious collaboration that settles in: "I won't call you out if you leave me alone." For example, when a partner turns their back on an affair because of the monetary advantages they find in the relationship, or when a boss overlooks an employee who is always late because the boss is doing the same, or when a food addict ignores a partner's excessive drinking to protect their own habit. This unconscious (or conscious) collusion does not build the kind of self-esteem that tenders respect for oneself or from others. Relationships are places to grow, not stagnate. Healthy relationships don't get their needs met elsewhere in unhealthy ways.

Respect Is Learned Early On

Children's thoughts and feelings can be either ignored or valued. When a child is asked about their preferences, they learn how to set boundaries. "Would you like a hug?" "Would you like to tell me how you feel?" "Did you and your brother work things out?" "Can you tell me why you dislike your teacher so much?" These questions show respect to a child and cause them to think about their own identity and how to respond. The more they practice sharing the innermost parts of themselves, the more natural it is to exercise mutual respect in relationships. They can state their preferences and acknowledge the needs of others as well. This is the preface to all negotiations throughout life.

Some people haven't learned the meaning of respect. They don't know how to take care of themselves, and they allow themselves to be used or vice versa. Like many of our distressing patterns, this is often a reenactment of behavior learned in childhood. We see it in people who didn't grow up feeling valued, weren't taught how to live a balanced life, or, as I've mentioned before, suffered a trauma that left them unhealed and wounded. These kids can become victims or perpetrators.

Take Jenny, for example. This patient of mine was raised in a family without structure and values. Her parents were divorced, and her mom was addicted to opiates. Her mom stayed up all night and slept all day. Jenny and her brother had a sitter who didn't supervise or enforce rules. There were no mealtimes, homework requirements, or sleeping schedules. She spent her night on the internet playing video games or chatting with strangers. Jenny was often late to school. Since she wasn't used to boundaries, she was regularly in trouble at school for being late to class, not completing assignments, and performing poorly.

By age fifteen, Jenny was skipping school to be with various guys she'd met online and started partying day and night. Even though she was used for sex and felt terrible about herself, she knew no way out of the maze. She was modeling her mother's behavior, and there was no motivation to change. Like so many families, the adults in her life targeted Jenny as the problem rather than recognizing how she became that way and how they enabled her to remain the same. Even when a school counselor or teacher tried to help her, she wouldn't keep her appointments. Her basic needs were met, so there was no incentive for her to change. Rarely can a therapist inspire a young adult to do better when the family system refuses to change their behaviors.

Jenny was a victim of childhood neglect, and ultimately—as someone who wasn't taught to respect herself or the environments on which she was dependent—she was a perpetrator. Without mutual respect for herself and those around her, she led a life swimming upstream against the current. While Jenny is an extreme example of someone who lives the *me program*, many people exhibit varying degrees of disregard for others. It's always important to be mindful that others deserve the same considerations and respect you want for yourself—the *we program*. Someone who is so self-absorbed that they only care about themselves and have little regard for how their behavior affects others is doomed to a life of conflict and disappointment. They take themselves out of the winner's circle.

♥

**There's a difference between being treated with respect
and actually being respected.**

There's a difference between being treated with respect and actually being respected. Just because someone is taught to respect others, doesn't mean they feel that way. This social protocol is a good skill, but it isn't necessarily authentic and won't hold up if not earned.

Respect, like trust, is earned. It's not something that is handed to someone. Being taken care of is not the way to self-respect. Learning how to take care of yourself and then helping others to learn independence is the way of love.

Sometimes, one person treats the other with respect, but it's not reciprocated. This is a victim-to-perpetrator relationship and can always be changed.

You Teach People How to Treat You

Self-respect is an inside job. It means you have integrity. You honor the legal and natural boundaries of life. Those with self-respect can be trusted. Their word is gold. They can be counted on to keep promises. They treat others like they want to be treated.

♥

Self-respect is an inside job.

Being treated poorly is a choice, and it's always a choice based on fear. If you don't respect yourself, you most likely don't know how. It's never too late to learn how to listen to the voice of love that will give you the right words and actions to achieve self-respect.

♥

Being treated poorly is a choice, and it's always a choice based on fear.

People who respect themselves have zero tolerance for abuse. When treated in an unkind or harmful manner, they will firmly and lovingly stick up for themselves. Rather than retaliate, they say something like, "I'd like to hear what you have to say but not in the way you're saying it. Let's be respectful to each other." If the abuse continues, they will disengage from the conversation: "I have to go now. Let's talk later when we're both calmer." If someone is physically abusive, the police are notified. Without consequences, this behavior will continue and often leads to death.

People with self-respect practice acceptance when things can't go as planned. For example, they let go of failed relationships, job pursuits that aren't working out, and anything else robbing them of their peace of mind. These people also have the internal fortitude to push through fear and resistance to accomplish their goals. They are relentless dream-seekers, without stepping on the toes of others. Because they are respectful, they have a loyal team to support them.

Self-respecters also know how to take care of themselves. They recognize that their human body is sacred, and they care for it as such. They exercise restraint when tempted to do something harmful to their physical well-being. They follow the rules but can bend them when it's in the best interests of everyone involved. They command their own ship and aren't subject to the whims of others. They will consider different points of view and then make educated choices that don't infringe on the rights of others. They are conscious of their actions and accept responsibility for them.

♥

Self-respect isn't about following rules.
It's about valuing them.

Sheila started therapy because she couldn't understand why she couldn't find a lasting relationship. She wanted to get married and have kids. She was educated and attractive but used sex to get men's attention and keep them hooked. She saw men as weak and seduced them with her sexy attire and flattery. The only problem was she found herself in situations where she didn't feel respected. Most of her encounters were one-night stands, but even when those evolved into relationships, they were turbulent. Her boyfriends often felt insecure about her seductive nature and questioned her loyalty. After one painful breakup, Sheila was on her knees, begging the voice of love for help. She was stunned by the response to her prayer: *You have more to offer than your looks. Try trust. Try revealing your real self.* It took a while for Sheila to find her truest self, a woman with great strength, determination, a sound mind, and a loving heart. She learned to get to know someone before she became intimate with them to see if they were a good fit for her instead of desperately seeking affirmation from other needy people. And instead of condemning herself for her past actions, she considered them learning experiences and turned those messes into the miracle of self-respect. Sheila didn't realize she was running on the fear of not being good enough. Once she chose to demonstrate self-respect, she began to attract like-minded people into her life. A few years later, a coworker introduced her to her future husband.

Self-respect isn't about following rules. It's about valuing them. The former is externally motivated and based on fear. The latter is internally motivated and based on love. Following rules out of fear of punishment is like being an emotionless robot. When rules are followed because you care about the well-being of other human beings, you feel good about yourself. Your motivation comes from a place of love instead of fear.

The Blame Game Never Works

It does no good to blame anyone, but you can hold people accountable. The best solution to any problem is to solve it. Let's imagine that you're in a situation where someone is treating you unkindly. Why are you accepting that behavior? Maybe you haven't been taught how to speak up for yourself. Perhaps you've been abused much of your life, and you don't know how to respond other than with avoidance. Or maybe you're choosing fear over love, and you fold when it comes to sharing your truth. If you don't want to be a victim, you can break this pattern once and for all. You must simply turn on the light.

... listen to the voice of love and let it guide you
through any situation.

First, be committed to learning how to respect yourself and others. Then you can listen to the voice of love and let it guide you through any situation. You can also find a therapist, coach, or spiritual advisor so that you have additional support. It's always good to get support when you are learning a new behavior, and it will help strengthen your resolve. By being coachable, you can learn just about anything.

When someone disrespects you, rather than ignoring the abuse or retaliating, find your voice of love and ask for the right words to address the conflict. Always wait until you feel neutral; otherwise, you're likely to fuel the fire rather than extinguish it. This is where most people get stuck. It's easier to fight when you're charged up, or what I refer to as "going nuclear." It takes courage to address a conflict calmly and lovingly.

Let's say your coworker has been taking supplies off your desk, and you've had enough of reaching for something only to find it gone. You're at the boiling point and have fantasies of telling the person off, but you know that could cause worse problems, so you stuff your feelings. After that, you start to dread seeing that person, seethe with resentment, and even obsess over ways to get even. If you decide to change your own behavior and approach the situation from a place of love, you can be the change that you want. For example, you could walk over to the employee's desk and say, "Hey, I notice my pen is on your desk. I'd like it back." The person will either hand it back and apologize or argue. In either case, you say, "Thanks so much for giving it back. I've noticed a lot of stuff missing off my desk, and it's pretty frustrating when I can't find what I need to get the job done."

♥

**. . . until you're ready to stick up for yourself,
you can't expect anyone else to look out for you.**

You don't have to win, and you don't have to be right. You simply speak your truth and leave it at that. You've made your point. If that doesn't work, you can develop a system to protect your things and lock them up.

You might feel yourself recoiling at this suggestion as it means you'd have to walk through your fear of confrontation. But until you're ready to stick up for yourself, you can't expect anyone else to look out for you.

Silence Isn't Always Golden

Let's go back to the two voices we talked about in the chapter on the first path. One voice wants to suppress you. It tells you to be quiet or else you might get fired, yelled at, or experience some type of conflict or loss. Once again, this voice is asking you to stuff down your feelings, feelings that will likely turn into suppressed anger and leave you feeling powerless. This voice keeps you in a state of feeling stuck and hopeless.

You can't go through life without experiencing anger, but it is a feeling you should promptly rid yourself of. When working with people, I tell them to write out their anger or pound pillows. I keep a plastic bat in my office that they pound on the sofa while screaming out their feelings. Once they discharge the toxic energy, they are calm and clearheaded. Sometimes, the anger completely subsides, and other times they must have a care-frontation (a loving conversation) to complete unfinished business.

The voice of love liberates you. It tells you to speak up without attacking or blaming anyone. If you listen to it and act accordingly, your conscience will be clear, and you will feel good about yourself. You won't need to project guilt onto anyone else. You could simply ask the other person to stop doing the unacceptable behavior. The goal of any conversation is to bring people closer together, but if the disrespect continues, you could merely disengage from the person or situation.

♥

If you feel like a victim, you must find your voice.

If you feel like a victim, you must find your voice. Then you're free to decide you're finished with that role, and you can allow the voice of love to guide you.

Ben, who had an eating disorder, started therapy for anxiety and depression. Whenever he felt that he didn't have control over his life, he followed a ritual. He'd order massive amounts of his favorite foods and binge until he felt like he was going to explode. He then forced himself to vomit. The rest of the evening and the following day, he'd feel sick from poisoning himself and violating the natural responses of his body. He'd feel depressed, and if he made it to work at all, he underperformed.

Ben knew he was an intelligent, capable person. He'd been able to achieve anything he'd set out to do. But he'd been stuck in a corporate tech career he didn't like and had been unable to break free. He felt he had gotten his job title without the respect of his associates. They didn't listen to him or care about his ideas, but it was himself he didn't appreciate. The more he learned to stick up for himself, the more Ben realized it wasn't a good fit for him to stay at the company. Rather than make that tough decision to leave his current career and follow the path of his dreams, he'd been trudging through each day and then punishing himself with binging and purging. Despite his confidence, Ben was stuck in a state of fear and suffered an inner loathing at his inability to break free.

Ben's healing moment happened one night when he saw himself holding on to the sides of the toilet and violently throwing up. As an observer, he heard that gentle inner voice: *You don't have to live like this anymore. There is another way.* Rather than dismissing the message, Ben realized what he had been doing. The lightbulb switched on, and he listened to the voice of love. Nothing but his own mind had been forcing him to stay in this imaginary hell. Now he could free himself from the bondage he'd voluntarily endured.

Over the next few months, Ben struggled with planning his exit strategy. "It's very emotional for me," he told me in our session. "I know I'll be all right, but I feel selfish about leaving. But what good am I if I don't want to be there anymore?"

Ben did not want to let anyone down and was torn between his inner calling and his guilt about leaving. Still, he knew he had to say goodbye for his own health, self-respect, and sense of self-worth. Within a month of his healing moment, he peacefully transitioned out of his executive position. He immediately started getting calls from people who respected his skill set and wanted to work with him. He gathered a team whose talents complemented one another, and together, they built Ben's dream business. Ben's life had been a mess, but by listening to the voice of love, the entire mess was transformed into a miracle. He had found the path to self-respect, which took him out of self-destructive habits and into the life he wanted.

The voice of love is always available, but unlike the voice of fear, it won't intrude on us. It will come across as a gentle suggestion, like with

Ben. He could have ignored it, but he chose to listen. Sometimes, we have to ask for the voice of love to guide us—*I'm not sure what to do; please help me*—then listen for the answer. It might come in fractured thoughts, or it might come in an intuitive action plan. You know when you've heard the voice of love because you have a sense of relief.

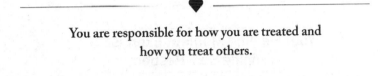

You are responsible for how you are treated and how you treat others.

As Shakespeare so clearly expressed in *Hamlet* through the words of Polonius. "To thine ownself be true . . . thou canst not then be false to any man."[1]

It's better to feel good about yourself and hold your head up high than succumb to the voice of fear and remain a victim.

You are responsible for how you are treated and how you treat others. When you treat yourself and others with kindness and consideration, you may not always be liked, but you will be respected. If you live in fear of what others think of you, you've sold yourself out. It's better to feel good about yourself and hold your head up high than succumb to the voice of fear and remain a victim. You may not know how to respect yourself, and it may not feel natural, but it's the same as learning any new language. This time, you're simply learning the language of respect by listening to the voice of love.

---   ♥   ---

You are the most important person you will ever respect.

You are the most important person you will ever respect.

Your Healing Moment Exercise 5:
Gaining Self-Respect

Once we learn self-respect, then that same behavior is carried to and from us. This exercise will help you to learn self-respect from a place of love instead of fear.

1. How would you define respect?

_____

_____

2. What were you taught about respect as a child? What things were helpful and not helpful? Were you given rules, or did someone explain how it feels good to treat one another with consideration?

_____

_____

_____

3. Write down how it feels to be treated respectfully.

_____

_____

4. How does it feel when you treat someone else with respect?

_____

_____

_____

5. Going forward, is there anything you could do to be more respectful to yourself and others?

_____

_____

_____

6. Are you willing to offer the same respect that you want to receive?

_____

_____

_____

7. What will it feel like to go through life respecting yourself and others?

_____

_____

_____

Three-Step Exercise for Respect

1. Imagine that you wake up tomorrow with a new attitude of respect for yourself and others.
2. Now visualize being with someone who isn't respectful.
3. Instead of being a victim to that person, how can you shift the narrative to earnestly show respect for yourself and that other person? Visualize the outcome that you would want to take place.

Chapter 6

SIXTH PATH: ABUNDANCE

You Are in Charge of Your Prosperity

To have all, give all, to all.
—*A Course in Miracles (Chapter 6)*

An onlooker once reprimanded me for giving money to a woman who approached me on the street. He said, "You're attracting bad people to the area; she's only going to buy drugs." I simply smiled at him and walked away. It wasn't my business what she did with the money. I was coming from love, not fear. Abundance, not lack.

Maybe you've heard the expression "You can't have it all." I remember thinking, *What part do I have to give up? Financial success, good friends, the perfect home, true love?* Fortunately, when I began to study *A Course in Miracles*, my perception changed. I realized there was no lack—of anything. Slowly, I learned that it was possible to have all these things.

Prosperity isn't just about money; it's also about having family, friends, and community involvement and fulfilling your purpose. It's about sharing whenever the opportunity presents itself.

♥

**Happiness is (wrongly) equated with getting the next
best thing—searching and never finding.**

Some people struggle their whole lives and never achieve financial security. Others have financial security but battle for love. In either case, it might seem that these things are being withheld. This is true, but not for the reasons one might think. We withhold these things from ourselves when guided by the voice of fear.

We've heard of people who have little material wealth yet lead happy lives. Happiness is (wrongly) equated with getting the next best thing—searching and never finding. We buy new cars and houses simply because it's time for a change. But how long until we stop noticing the fine leather seats, the dazzling dashboard, or the super-slick rims?

♥

. . . things cannot be a replacement for love.

Clearly, there's no long-term satisfaction in the ongoing quest for more. There's nothing wrong with wanting nice things; it's perfectly normal and healthy. But things cannot be a replacement for love. Until your focus shifts from receiving to sharing, the journey for fulfillment will be misguided. Instead of achieving a deep sense of purpose, you'll get a huge mess—more debt, more disappointment, and, even worse, a deeper void. But you can turn that sense of emptiness into an abundance mindset.

Transcending the Dependency/Receiving Phase

People stuck in the dependency phase have been trained in how to receive but not in how to give. Prosperity requires sharing and receiving. People who've been overly dependent on parents or other caretakers suffer extreme trauma when forced to stand on their own or be financially self-sufficient. They feel like they've been abandoned on a deserted island without a compass, map, or guide. Overcome with terror, they often fail to see they are quite capable of self-care and autonomy. Even full-grown adults frantically ask, "Why can't she see what I need?" "Why don't they understand I just want a little help?" "What am I supposed to do with myself?"

♥

Keeping another person dependent is like slowly but surely sabotaging their life force.

Someone who remains dependent always has an enabler. Unfortunately, those who enable others are also living in fear. They think that something terrible will happen to the person they love (or themselves) if they let go. One patient, Rick, at age forty, was terrified to move out of his parents' house. He was overcome with the guilt at the thought of abandoning his parents even though they were financially secure and healthy. He'd been the glue that kept his family together. Moving meant his parents might get a divorce, and he unconsciously felt responsible for keeping them together. For some people, it's too scary to confront the cycle of dependence. Ironically, the longer the dependency continues, the more disabled their loved one becomes. Keeping another person dependent is like slowly but surely sabotaging their life force. Then, when an enabler is no longer available, the dependent loved one is left in a state of paralyzing despair. At that point, the feared crisis is real but of the enabler's own making. Rick's healing moment came when he realized it wasn't healthy for him or his family for him to be the conduit that held things together. It was time for him to find his own life and for his parents to face their own issues.

Babies Have to Receive; Children Learn to Share

From the moment of birth, we've been taught to receive. Babies can't survive without total care. Over time, the baby is encouraged to become more independent and, ultimately, a self-sufficient adult who can care for and be cared for—interdependency. There's always enough to eat, affection, and time in an abundant household. Children who've suffered a lack of these things tend never to feel satisfied, and they're always hungry for whatever's missing. There's no perfect scenario, but it must be good enough to prevent a sense of lack. There are also reasonable limits. Children can understand that they can't have everything. As they get older, they also are taught how to earn what they want (like allowance) and how to contribute to their household (like chores).

Since most relationships, regardless of form, are give-and-take, unilateral giving rarely works long-term. When one person does most of the receiving, the relationship becomes unbalanced. Like a bank account, when energy is withdrawn without being replenished, the balance eventually hits zero.

One of my closest friends suffered a tragic divorce because she'd not been taught this concept. An only child, she'd been pampered her whole life, groomed to be a trophy wife. Her parents did without so that she could have exposure to a first-class life: the best schools, clothes, culture, and anything else she wanted. But when she married a man just starting his career, she agreed on the role of housewife without having any tools to fulfill those responsibilities or the funds to acquire someone to help her. Her day consisted of coffee, cigarettes, magazines, and going to the beach.

Furthermore, despite having the best education, she didn't have an employable skill. The tipping point occurred after the birth of their child. She could hardly care for their baby and often slept through night-time and morning feedings. Her husband pleaded with her that he was overwhelmed and couldn't manage all that he was doing. Several family members warned her that she needed to take more interest in the home and the baby, but she couldn't heed the warnings. I tried everything to help my friend. It grieved me to see her needlessly suffer. She simply couldn't comprehend what she was doing wrong. Digging deep within herself to give back, even to her own benefit, was so foreign to her that it was impossible. Her husband had already been the provider, the cook, the housekeeper, and now he was changing diapers, making bottles, functioning sleep-deprived, and arriving late to work. After her husband filed for divorce, he left her and the baby, and my friend was emotionally shattered, alone, and still unable to understand why her marriage failed.

Her inability to commit her energy to the relationship left her feeling abandoned and barely able to survive. Soon after, out of desperation, she met someone else and remarried. The marriage lasted, but the problems she brought with her remained.

Every person has a talent and a gift to share with others.

It's one thing when someone honestly cannot care for themselves. They may have limited choices and genuinely need assistance. However, even people with severe disabilities contribute to their families, to their friends, and to their employers. Some even start their own businesses. But those who have a fear-based dependency have developed a phobic-type of reaction to being self-sufficient. They are unable to take the first steps to move through the discomfort of change as the voice of fear has led them to complacency.

Whatever your role, everyone has a purpose.

Besides being totally reliant, these individuals are missing out on their life's purpose. Every person has a talent and a gift to share with others. Maybe you're destined to be a famous singer or the best mom imaginable. Whatever your role, everyone has a purpose. Most people take their talents and convert them to serving or enriching others in some way. Even more important, they are fulfilling their mission.

Anyone who's stuck in the role of being dependent can change. It might be challenging to become self-sufficient later in life, but it's not impossible. It's never too late to grow up.

———————————— ♥ ————————————

It might be challenging to become self-sufficient later in life, but it's not impossible. It's never too late to grow up.

First, you must remove any barriers that are blocking your success. For example, if you are preoccupied with some behavior that's draining your energy, you must first remedy that problem. If you can't do this yourself, get help and stick with it until you feel well enough to face the world.

Next, focus on accomplishing whatever tasks are essential to meet your goal. Some people finish their degrees, get trained in new skills, or start home businesses. They push themselves out into the mainstream of society through social events so that they can network. And they get support from a mentor or coach for objective input and accountability. Happy people thrive on doing what they love.

———————————— ♥ ————————————

Happy people thrive on doing what they love.

Last, give back to others what you have received—pay it forward. Be ready to help someone who needs guidance like you did. I remember how hard I struggled when I started my psychotherapy career. Fortunately, I had a good mentor who helped me make the best decisions to attract patients. Because of his generosity and guidance, I have always paid it forward when a student or intern comes to me for help.

Every career has value to the well-being of others. Chefs, gardeners, lawyers, musicians, postal carriers, rocket scientists, and waste managers all make life easier for those around them by serving or directing them or providing solutions to problems. And whether they serve their families, their neighborhood, their country, or their continent, their contributions help the planet thrive and make the world a better place to live. Our planet isn't that different from an ant or bee colony. Every role is equally vital for the good of all.

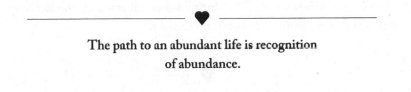

The path to an abundant life is recognition
of abundance.

No Lack of Time, Money, or People

The path to an abundant life is recognition of abundance. You always have an abundance of creativity—the fiber of plentiful. Many people's fears are driven by a sense of scarcity, a lack of what they want. The greater their worries, the more they withhold. But when you withhold from others, you limit the pipeline to yourself. Limited thinking blocks the possibility of seeing greater opportunities.

Focusing on a lack of time or money, even when someone has more than enough of both, is a condition of fear-based thinking. Charles Dickens described an extreme example of this dilemma in his novella, *A Christmas Carol*. The main character, Scrooge, was portrayed as a miserly, greedy, self-absorbed businessman who withheld every bit of his money and time from others. It wasn't until the Ghosts of Christmas descended upon him and forced him to face his pain and fears that he was freed from the past and able to love. Consequently, he opened his heart to his devoted employee, Bob Cratchit, and bountifully bestowed upon Cratchit's family much-needed food and money, and medical care for his son Tiny Tim. While Scrooge had all the time and money, he had a life of misery. Once he learned to give, he had all the love he could want.[1]

Most people have at least a little Scrooge in them. We try to hang on to what we have. The thought of letting go of our hard-earned money is usually met with resistance. (Unless it's for something we want, and then caution goes to the wind). To sum it up, *A Course in Miracles* teaches there is no lack of money, only fear-based, limited thoughts, a lack of creative ideas. Most of our fears are self-fulfilling. Fear of lack begets lack. But the more we give, the more we receive. The stock market, for instance, runs on people's fears. People don't want to buy when the market is down because they fear a permanent crash. They don't want to sell when the market is up because they don't want to miss out on the gains.

♥

**Fear of lack begets lack. But the more we give,
the more we receive.**

Think of money like anything else you want to grow. Imagine every month you get a supply of potatoes. The end of the month rolls around, and you only have three potatoes left. What if that's all the food you have for the next three days? You can portion them out and make them last until you receive your next bag of potatoes, or you can decide to do something else. You can take one of the potatoes, cut out the eyes, and use them to grow other potatoes. You'll lose some of your current supply, but soon, you will not only have your monthly supply but extra potatoes as well. If you do this every month, you'll eventually have more potatoes than you could possibly consume. You then can either hoard your potatoes or share them with other people and teach them the same technique. When you give away what you have, it keeps growing. Now everyone has gone from a limited supply to an unlimited supply. Simply by letting go of a few potatoes every month, everyone can live in abundance.

♥

When you give away what you have, it keeps growing.

So, we see that there never was a lack of potatoes; it only seemed that way. When we get locked into thinking of less, we shut down the possibility of more. When we stop listening to the voice of fear and tune in to our creative side, though, all kinds of new ideas can present themselves.

I was scared after my second divorce. I didn't have a job. I had enough money to last a few months, but I knew I needed to find employment. I went on multiple job interviews but was either passed over or offered a salary that wasn't enough to provide for my family. I was discouraged that I'd made more money as a waitress than it seemed I could with a master's degree. It took all my effort to fight off the heebie-jeebies, but I continued to trust that things would work out, despite the evidence to the contrary. Memories of my first divorce kept haunting me, living with a baby in a roach-filled apartment with barely enough money for food. But that mess was what had motivated me to go to college and get a better life. I just kept affirming that was then, and this was now.

Almost out of money and with no more interviews scheduled, I just kept affirming there was a plan, and it would be revealed to me—and it was. Soon, I ran into a colleague in a coffee shop. We'd often brainstormed about sharing a counseling service, and now we decided to implement a plan. We volunteered our time in the community doing mental health presentations on depression and bereavement. We rented a room from a psychologist at his office and started our own support groups for people going through divorce. Soon, we saw those patients on an individual basis. Then, these patients referred other people to us. Once we could afford it, we rented our own office. We continued to give back to the community through time and small donations. Within a year, we had more business than we could accommodate. The mess of having no work turned into a miracle of abundance, all from listening to the voice of love instead of the voice of fear.

---------------------------------- ♥ ----------------------------------

No matter how bad things may seem, there's always an opportunity to turn messes into miracles.

No matter how bad things may seem, there's always an opportunity to turn messes into miracles. During the COVID pandemic, many chose possibility over terror. Some businesses shifted to virtual meetings, resulting in less traveling time, fewer expenses, and increased profits. With food delivery services and online retailers, customers found they could purchase most things on the internet and enjoy the convenience and safety of staying home. Due to the demand for these services, stocks in these companies grew at alarming rates, presenting a good investment opportunity. Telemedicine and teletherapy have risen to astronomical proportions as well, making those services easier for everyone to access, no matter their degree of mobility.

Some individuals used the COVID shutdown to transform from employee to entrepreneur. Life and fitness coaches and home services sprang up everywhere. Innovators created apps that provided relaxation, meditation, and therapy to help people cope with stress. Some people found new income by selling their items online. I transformed my psychotherapy practice into a concierge service that provided an entirely new approach to treatment and better care. It's designed for people who need intensive outpatient treatment but who want privacy not available in an institutional setting. Aside from extensive psychotherapy, a conduit for necessary resources, and twenty-four-hour availability, the patient's support system is encouraged to participate in the program.

These are just a few examples of turning messes into miracles through adopting an abundance mindset rich with possibility. For some, this increased ability to help others led to an abundance of time and the ability to give back to those suffering the genuine economic consequences of the pandemic.

Spiritual Economics

Sharing time and money are acts of love. When you are sharing those gifts, you are receiving them as well—monetarily and emotionally—in direct proportion to your output.

Maybe you've heard the expression "if you need to get something done, ask a busy person." Achievers know how to manage their time efficiently yet generously. They don't feel a lack of time because they don't waste it. Instead of having the to-do list hanging over their heads, they just have a *do* list, and they do it now. By addressing things as they come up, they aren't weighed down with ever-growing piles of paperwork, phone calls, and errands. Instead, they are freed to enjoy the rest of their precious moments unencumbered with thoughts like *too many tasks, so little time.*

♥

Sharing time and money are acts of love.

There's a difference between being wealthy and experiencing abundance. Some people get rich, but they don't reap a life of abundance. Abundance is not only wealth but also feeling a sense of fullness that comes from sharing the wealth. Those who think abundantly (regardless of their income) pay their bills on time, minimize debt, and save for emergencies so that they don't feel pressure from an unexpected crisis. Their credit score is golden because a good score equals power. They keep part of the money to enjoy as a reward for their labors. They make regular and consistent donations because the more they share, the more their garden grows. This includes contributions to individuals in need and for whom there is no tax write-off—but even if there is a tax advantage, the universe puts it in the giver's plus column. We can share all the time—extra tipping, anonymously helping to pay for someone else's education, secretly picking up someone's tab in a restaurant, offering your expertise free of charge, or sending a cashier's check to a family in need.

♥

**Abundance is not only wealth but also feeling a sense of
fullness that comes from sharing the wealth.**

---------------------------- ♥ ----------------------------

Just as a mighty oak must drop its acorns to produce
other mighty oaks, giving away money plants seeds
of future growth.

There are numerous books on spiritual economics, and they all
describe the benefits of tithing, giving 10 percent or more of your income
to a worthy cause. People like Scrooge who hold on to money may become
rich, but they are missing spiritual fulfillment. Just as a mighty oak must
drop its acorns to produce other mighty oaks, giving away money plants
seeds of future growth. Financial prosperity and spiritual prosperity are
synonymous.

Spiritual economic gurus such as Napoleon Hill teach the value of
utilizing creative skills and then turning them into monetary reality. Hill
teaches his students to tap into their natural gifts and develop a plan to
capitalize on those talents and then provides basic steps to implement the
dream.

---------------------------- ♥ ----------------------------

Financial prosperity and spiritual prosperity
are synonymous.

Andy, at age twenty-five, had a dream of financial prosperity. After
studying Hill's book *Think and Grow Rich*,[2] Andy developed a plan to stop
working as an electrical employee and start his own electrical business.
First, he quit his job so that he could study for his contractor's license.
Then, he followed the steps outlined by Hill. He passed the final licensing
exam, bought a used van, printed some business cards, and made calls to
potential customers. He had an office, ten employees, and grossed more

than one million in annual income within two years. His fearless endeavor turned his dream into a living-color experience.

You can have what you want; you need only plant a healthy garden, tend to it, wait for it to grow, and then share it with others.

♥

You can have what you want; you need only plant
a healthy garden, tend to it, wait for it to grow,
and then share it with others.

No Lack of Romantic Love Either

The fear of never having a life partner drives some people to desperate lengths. One of my therapist friend's favorite mantras was "There are no good men left; they're all married. The rest are alcoholics or narcissists." Unfortunately, her belief outlived her, and she died alone. But not from trying. During our ten-year acquaintance, she hooked up with more men than a casino has chips. She acted out her pain and fears by using sex to feel validated while lacking belief in her ability to have an authentic relationship. When I pointed out to her that there was no lack (rejecting her scarcity mindset) and that there were always quality partners to be found, she scoffed at my "naivete."

♥

. . . happy people generally aren't lonely,
regardless of their relationship status.

It's easy to look around and see everyone else in a happy relationship while you're all alone. But consider this: happy people generally aren't lonely, regardless of their relationship status. And contrary to popular belief, not all men want a beautiful, younger woman, and not all women want a rich man. Those who prioritize beauty or wealth in romantic partners have been conditioned to do so and are often attempting to fill a void in themselves. If they learned to find beauty in everyone and achieved their own mission and purpose, they would be much closer to authentic love. And this is precisely why so many people at all socioeconomic levels, ages, and appearances find true love every day.

♥

The person who sits around wishing for something to happen will get just that: lots of wishes.

If you want true love, you must get out of the invisible box in which you live. Boxes are places to hide. Rather than waiting for your box to be filled by another, get out and give back to your friends and community. Pick a hobby or a volunteer project so that you can meet new people. Be helpful to others. This principle is the same as the others; the more you give, the more you receive. Before you realize it, your box will be more than full.

The person who sits around wishing for something to happen will get just that: lots of wishes. The person who is involved in having fun and helping others is a magnetic force. Jim met his true love through his father, who introduced him to a co-board member at a nonprofit agency. Greg met his life partner when he signed up for choir at his church. Seventy-something Molly met her soul mate when she was selling her house, and he teased that he'd purchase it, but only if she came with the house. My husband and I met at a volunteer group business meeting.

Relationships are not the path to happiness, but people are the most in-demand when they are on a path to happiness and have something to share. Instead of looking for someone to love them, they've learned how to love themselves and give back to others. If you walk around with an empty box looking for someone to fill it, you'll likely meet someone with another empty box.

♥

There are people all around you longing for friendship and who would love to spend time together.

If you genuinely want to share and receive love with a like-minded partner, focus on the obstacles that are preventing you from self-fulfillment. In other words, what do you want from a partner, and how can you provide more of that to yourself? Start with a list of your fears and address them one by one. If loneliness is consuming you, walk through that fear to the nearest social event, even if it's simply talking to a new neighbor. Then start offering to do something for that new friend. Next, suggest you do some type of group activity together. Apply the same effort to other people you work or live near. There are people all around you longing for friendship and who would love to spend time together. Do volunteer work. Start a new hobby that involves meeting new people. Soon, you'll have a whole new support system.

Sometimes the barriers to adopting an abundant view of our self-worth, and of ourselves as worthy partners, are more challenging than we can handle alone. If your heart's been broken and you're afraid of being hurt again, get some help to work through the pain so that you can free yourself from your past. If you're substituting alcohol, drugs, food, or some other dependency or addiction for a loving relationship, replace it with an activity that improves your self-esteem. (See the appendix 77+ Ways to Self-Love at the end of this book.) The more you choose to love, the fuller your box becomes.

If It's Not Happening, Who's Waiting on Whom?

Sometimes, we do all the right things, and it still seems like nothing's happening or moving in the direction we want. It's important to remember that just because you don't see your garden grow doesn't mean it's not. The same is true when planting seeds of love and prosperity. It takes time to see the long-term results. Just keep pulling the weeds.

Meanwhile, during these slower growing periods, you can continue to work on yourself. Focus on developing patience and trust, reflecting on the past, and developing a perspective that lets you see outside yourself.

───────────────── ♥ ─────────────────

. . . when planting seeds of love and prosperity.
It takes time to see the long-term results.
Just keep pulling the weeds.

───────────────────────────────

When I'm in the waiting rooms of life, I like to do a personal inventory. I ask, "What might I be doing that's interfering with success?" Sometimes I've forgotten to share my time and money. Or perhaps I've treated someone unlovingly. What if I'm in the waiting room so I can look beyond my life and see what it feels like on the other side of the fence? Sometimes I realize I've failed to remember something I was supposed to do and that my oversight is holding someone else up. Once I take care of my business, the flow resumes.

These time-outs have been a powerful experience and an elixir that unclogs my spiritual pipeline and fills it with newfound insights. They are often preceded with the loving voice that says, "I was wondering when you were going to realize that the universe was waiting on you, not the other way around."

───────────────── ♥ ─────────────────

A gratitude mindset makes it hard to feel
deprived or depressed.

───────────────────────────────

It's also important to be grateful. In the quest for abundance, it's easy to take things for granted. A gratitude mindset makes it hard to feel deprived or depressed. Make it a daily practice to look around you and say thank you for all that has been bestowed upon you.

Your prosperity is the direct result of your own consciousness, your own behaviors, and your own willingness to embrace a model of abundance. When you implement your creative ideas and share your profits with others, there is no limit to what you can achieve. Your fearless endeavors will cut your path to success. So, choose to do what you love, and love will do the rest.

You are the one in control of your prosperity.

Your Healing Moment Exercise 6:
Prosperity Consciousness

Abundance is directly related to your consciousness and how you demonstrate a sense of lack (fear) or plenty (love). These exercises will help you to understand your mindset and how to increase your prosperity.

1. Did your role models demonstrate a life of abundance or lack? How did this affect you?

   _____

   _____

   _____

2. In which area (if any) do you feel a sense of lack? Money, time, love? When did you first feel this sense of lack?

   _____

   _____

   _____

3. Concerning the three areas in question two, which one(s) would you like to have abundance in?

   _____

   _____

   _____

4. Based on this chapter, what steps would accomplish your goals in question three? What purpose are you here to fulfill? With whom can you share your time and money?

_____

_____

_____

5. Are you willing to be patient and learn to develop spiritual muscle when things aren't happening as fast as you'd like? How will you modify your behavior to accomplish this?

_____

_____

_____

6. List any fears you have concerning giving your time and money.

_____

_____

_____

7. Are you willing to take a leap of faith?

_____

_____

_____

Three-Step Exercise for Abundance

1. Close your eyes and visualize what your life would look like if it were abundant.
2. Now close your eyes again and dream an even bigger dream.
3. Take a large piece of white construction paper and make a vision board. You do this by cutting out pictures in magazines, taking photos, or writing down your greatest dreams—things you want to manifest in your life. Keep adding to your board. Pull it out every once in a while and see what has materialized.

Chapter 7

SEVENTH PATH: SELF-LOVE

No One Will Love You More than You Love Yourself

You have so little faith in yourself because you are unwilling
to accept the fact that perfect love is in you, and so you seek
without for what you cannot find within.
—*A Course in Miracles (Chapter 5, VI)*

Many of us have made the huge mistake of thinking that love is something you find. Nothing could be further from the truth. When you seek love, you can spend your entire life searching for something that you already have. This is the same problem as searching for God "out there." To find love or God, you must journey inward. You must learn to love yourself, on your own, as you are in this moment.

No one will love you more than you love yourself.

Some people wait their whole life for true love. We've been conditioned to think that the ultimate love story will make life complete. Romeo and Juliet and their unbridled feelings for each other set the bar for how we view romance—and it's a confusing bar at best. Love songs and movies continuously reinforce the notion that passionate, undying love will make everything perfect. Some people live to fulfill that fantasy. When it doesn't turn out like the movies or songs, they feel sorely disillusioned.

When marriage doesn't provide enough fulfillment, many parents find gratification through their children. *At least my kids love me,* they think. These parents live to watch their kids succeed as a reflection and extension of themselves. When the child breaks away or does the opposite of what the parent thinks is best, the parent feels hurt and disappointed. Once again, love is associated with pain instead of gratification.

No one will love you more than you love yourself.

Some people try to find love through friendships. We want to feel connected. We don't want to be the one on the outside watching everyone else having fun. We hear about best friends forever who always have each other's back. We search for a "bestie" in the hopes of having that special bond. Then, when someone doesn't live up to our expectations or betrays us, we suffer. We walk away from the friendship and mourn the loss. Once again, we are disillusioned and alone.

Many people search for love through their careers. They devote endless hours to work and often achieve great fulfillment from their accomplishments. But a job and all its benefits don't mean much without others with whom to share. Some of the wealthiest and most successful people ache with an emptiness that cannot be satiated with all the riches that money can buy.

. . . religion is not love or God.

Other people try to find a God to love them. They go to religious institutions, sometimes jumping from one sect to the next, thinking one religion is better than another. They may learn new skills and have better lives, but religion is not love or God.

All too often, these failed dreams lead to pain and sorrow. It can seem like the world is full of selfish people who care only about themselves. We might give up on finding love and fill the void with substitutes—alcohol, drugs, food, pills, sex, smoking, and multiple other ways to suppress our never-ending ache. You might think you love these things because of how they make you feel. But they are often substitutes for love. Unnatural highs might temporarily feel good, but they are anything but loving. Our bodies are sacred temples that house our spirits, not places to be used as toxic waste dumps. Our minds are here to be creative and fulfill a mission. But when we search for love in all the wrong places, we don't find heaven or our purpose. Instead, we find hell.

♥

Our minds are here to be creative and fulfill a mission.

I have made all these mistakes and even more, but love turned those messes into miracles.

Born to Love

Here's how it works. For the entire gestation period, a baby is in a warm, safe environment. There's plenty of supply for all the baby's needs. Once the baby enters the world, their needs must be met. If there's a satisfactory transition from in utero to outside life, the baby is still in want of nothing. There's plenty of food, nurturing, and cuddling. This is not equated to love yet, but as time goes on, an insufficiency of these things can correlate to unworthiness. Of course, there are lots of families who struggle. But some of these parents make do with what they have, and the kids are helped to understand why they have less than others—it's not internalized. Their tummies are still full, the climate feels good, they feel safe, and there are lots of hugs and affirmations.

There's a reasonable amount of discipline, but usually nonphysical, such as brief time-outs. Most importantly, parents talk to their children lovingly about their behavior and why it's essential to have a cooperative attitude toward others and their environment. They don't yell at or shame them. If they do, they apologize. There are consequences for violating boundaries, but they are educational, not punitive. For example, if a child steals from a sibling, they must apologize and pay it back. If they fail to do their chore, they have to do double duty next time.

♥

*People who don't feel loved endeavor on an endless
search to find a missing piece of their heart.*

Children don't need a perfect world. That would be harmful and wouldn't equip the child for misfortunes and harsh realities. Too much doting and accommodation leads a child to think they are entitled to have everything go their way. But when a child does not feel wanted or cared for, or is abused, they have not learned that they are loveable. As the child grows, their compass takes them to all the wrong places in an attempt to find something they think they don't have. People who don't feel loved endeavor on an endless search to find a missing piece of their heart.

Whether you feel loved or unloved, the only place to find the missing piece is right inside yourself.

♥

*Whether you feel loved or unloved, the only place to
find the missing piece is right inside yourself.*

Looking for Love in All the Wrong Places

My dream since childhood was to go to college, get married, have kids, and live happily ever after, just like in the fairy tales. My family tried to program me to believe that I was beautiful and intelligent and could have anyone I wanted. Since I didn't feel like these things were true, this only made me depressed. Instead of teaching children that looks are important and using their physical assets as bait to attract the opposite sex, we could teach them that love and marriage are about compatibility, growth, and contributing to the world around them. Relationships are about sharing and receiving love. A place to heal the past when old wounds emerge. A haven for friends and family when they are hurting.

♥

Relationships are about sharing and receiving love.

Most of my good impressions came from television shows portraying the idyllic family. Despite mistakes and conflicts, these families show love and concern for each other. Children learn from their own parents' modeling. Children who see parents appropriately affectionate with one another, working together as a team, calmly problem-solving, being sober of mind, and spending time as a family are more likely to make better choices. Parents who take time to explain the reasons for rules and practice what they preach are helping their kids to internalize a value system. Kids raised in a stable, loving environment feel secure and are equipped to go into the world and build their own healthy relationships.

I never had a good image of marriage. I didn't want to copy my role models' marriages. Instead, I wanted a wholesome relationship, whatever that meant, but at least no fighting, no drinking, a place where my kids would feel safe and happy. But not having a clue how to bypass my early image meant it took a lot of healing, practice, and multiple marriages to get it right.

None of my fantasies materialized; they were thwarted by my misplaced attempts for love, starting with my first cigarette at age twelve. When the nicotine hit my brain, I had a sense of well-being for the first time in my life. This was my first substitute for love. Later, alcohol took me out of my painful shyness and feelings of inferiority. My next brilliant decision was to marry at age sixteen to get out of my dysfunctional family and start my own. Two years later, I was divorced with an eighteen-month-old child.

My vision of going away to a big university was quashed. Instead, I managed to go to night school to earn a high school diploma and then a community college degree. I juggled single parenting with school and my waitressing job. Teenage single parenting was hard. I tried family therapy, but it didn't help me or my child. Alcohol was never addressed.

I wasn't smart enough to recognize that addiction hindered my brain's ability to make good decisions—the thought of being addicted never crossed my mind. I just had a few bad habits. I saw alcoholism as drinking day and night, racking up DUIs, and continuing to drink no matter how much you lost—the type of alcoholism I'd witnessed growing up. I never suffered health or legal consequences. And no one suggested I had a problem, so I remained in denial. I didn't know that I was an addict, and that addiction is a silent killer, like slowly administering rat poisoning. By the time the symptoms are apparent, it's too late. It takes a skilled and experienced professional to recognize the signs early on. Unfortunately, none of my therapists were that.

Eventually, my bad decisions led to the emotional combustion that brought me to a screeching halt, and I finally got help. It was easy to stop drinking, but smoking was an entirely different challenge. I quit and started dozens of times. The light switched on when someone told me, "When you love yourself as much as you love cigarettes, you'll be able to quit." So, I quit, but without understanding the nature of addiction or love. I simply replaced cigarettes with compulsive exercise, a new relationship, another spiritual journey, or anything else that would produce the high.

Included among my addictions were decades of therapy. I worked and worked on myself. It eased the pain but didn't fill the deep, dark void inside of me. I still was not learning how to love myself. On top of that, bad things kept happening—cancer, deaths, fires, hurricanes. Every time I'd get up, another crisis would knock me down. I kept searching and could not find the love I so desperately wanted.

I didn't realize that the God and the love I sought were not "out there." Meanwhile, my silent pain was eating me alive.

I was unknowingly serving two masters. Part of me was committed to doing the right things in life, while the other part sabotaged me every step of the way. I'd studied *A Course in Miracles* for twenty years, and I knew all about the two voices, but I'd never realized that I was the queen of equally obeying both. I couldn't see that the voice of fear had buried me deeper and deeper into the abyss.

A relapse was inevitable.

I embarked on a two-year spree of rebellious and outrageous behaviors. Yes, indeed. I was as crazy as a witch on a spinning broom.

It took another internal meltdown before God got my attention.

One late night after an incredibly disappointing day, I drove off the road and into a hedge. Stunned, I pulled the car into an abandoned parking lot. Sitting alone, I looked out of the windshield and felt as black as the night sky, void of light. I'd had enough alcohol and pills to dysregulate my emotions and suddenly found myself uncontrollably sobbing.

Through racking sobs, I railed at God, "What do you want from me? I've tried everything to get well and be a better person! You probably don't even exist, and if you do, you obviously don't care about me."

And then, like an invisible slap partly to get my attention but mainly to shut me up, I heard the matter-of-fact answer to my absurd question.

Donna. It's not me who doesn't love you. You don't love yourself.

I was dumbstruck. The message shot through my denial, and light flooded into my delusional thinking. I knew it was the truth—this was my healing moment. I'd always believed that if I did all the right things, a magical God would wave his wand and fulfill my wishes. I thought about whether what I wanted was good for me but quickly dismissed any concerns. I just wanted what I wanted, and God was supposed to deliver. When it came to relationships, if everyone around me told me a person wasn't right for me, I just assumed they weren't spiritual enough to see the relationship's potential. I thought I'd turned my life and my will over to the care of God, but I'd only been playing a game of spiritual chess against myself. My life and decisions would have been entirely different if I'd loved myself. But I couldn't change the past. I didn't even want to. As I sat in the car flooded with these truths, I realized how blind I'd been.

The next day, when I woke up, I felt like a different person. I didn't care about anything but getting to a recovery meeting. I started over again, but this time, with a whole different consciousness, I knew I belonged.

I'd been so blind that once the light turned on, I was disorientated. Like a bear coming out of hibernation, I had to find nourishment. Now that I'd heard the truth, what was I going to do about it? I didn't love myself, but what did that mean? *I didn't have a clue how to love myself or anyone else.* Dealing with people felt like fighting off stinging bees to get to the honey. I'd rather do without.

♥

**If you want love, be the love that you want,
and you will have it.**

My spirituality needed a complete overhaul. That magician was still lingering in the back of my mind, and it had to be replaced with reality. I had to learn to love myself. I didn't find God in churches, temples, Indian spiritual sites, psychedelics, or sacred shrines. The closest I'd ever felt to a divine presence was out on the ocean or on a mountain peak. I suspected this was because when in those peaceful settings, the noise in my head subsided, and I could feel in these moments of solitude and silence a connection with God in everything. I attempted to forget everything I'd previously learned about spirituality and love. My mind wasn't capable of grasping what I wanted to understand—it was too all-encompassing. I thought about the divine intelligence that kept everything together. There had to be a master design that we could work with or against.

One day while in quiet contemplation, a thought came to me: *If you want love, be the love that you want, and you will have it.* I felt the resistance well up inside of me. The responsibility was being placed squarely on my own shoulders. How annoying. I'd much prefer God to be in charge. I couldn't deny the truth of the thought, though: I had to be the one in control of how much love I would offer and receive. I didn't need to get love. I already had it. The only path to love was to be loving.

♥

Now, rather than get love, I had to learn how to be love.

This awareness entirely changed my perception. I'd always chased feelings. They were something I sought and never felt better. Consequently, I didn't realize I was getting high on feelings that had nothing to do with love. No wonder I was substituting love with addiction. Now, rather than getting love, I had to learn how to be love.

My actions had to change first. But how? Another awareness descended upon me: *There's a seed in me that operates under the same principle as any other seed.* I could either leave the seed in the package or plant it in fertile soil and give it the nourishment it needed to thrive. Once in the ground, I couldn't just walk away either; I needed to stand in and tend it. My spirituality could grow the same way—replacing the voice of fear that would rob my peace of mind (pulling the weeds) with the voice of love (nourishing the garden).

♥

Love wasn't something I'd ever acquire because I already had all the love that I needed.

I had learned in *A Course in Miracles* that love will find itself,[1] and I was beginning to understand that idea. Love wasn't something I'd ever acquire because I already had all the love that I needed. But the only way to access that love was to emanate love, which would attract love to me. Now in the position of being love itself, my search was over.

It was then that I realized that love is an action word. When a baby cries, you don't yell from another room, "I love you!" You might have loving feelings toward the baby, but love means you get up (whether you feel like it or not) and tend to the baby. When the baby is upset, you give them the appropriate remedy for their needs. You certainly don't hand the baby a cigarette, a needle full of heroin, a shot of vodka, a porn video, or a bag of jellybeans. Instead, you provide a loving and safe environment so that the baby can form a secure attachment to you.

. . . love is an action word.

You act with love, and then the feelings come. I had to take care of myself the same way. That meant eating healthy, balancing work and play and exercise and rest, apologizing when wrong, staying away from mean people (even if they were family), saying my prayers, expressing feelings in a healthy way, helping people who wanted it, and getting into myself to get out of myself.

The change in me was so fast that I could hardly believe it. I felt happy for the first time in my life. I was glad to wake up in the morning and slept peacefully at night. Many heavy things were going on (employee theft, family conflicts, and unexpected expenses), but they did not dominate my thoughts or interfere with my serenity. Love meant being patient, letting life unfold.

Love doesn't force itself.

I became willing to patch things up in relationships I'd damaged with my relapse. Some recovered, some did not, and that was okay. Love doesn't force itself. Relationships are unsalvageable unless both people forgive themselves and each other.

Then another thought came to me: *You can't lose a friend you never had.* I digested that and realized that without forgiveness, there is no friendship. At some point in time, people always disappoint one another, and forgiveness is the only way to heal those harms.

I became mindful of all my blessing, like the cozy covers, fluffy pillows, running water, songbirds, paint, shelter, and shelves stocked with books—things that I'd taken for granted in my addiction. Old projects were finished, even my first book; it was a total flop, but that didn't matter, and it spurred me on to write the next.

Daily prayer and meditation resumed without any expectations other than giving that time to silence. I now enjoyed the recovery meetings with a new state of mind. I made a point of sitting next to those who formerly annoyed me, and I offered them kindness. I adopted a new dad in the meetings. Bill was a gentle and clear thinker with rock-solid recovery skills. He and his wife became close friends, and he gave me the paternal guidance I'd always lacked and sorely needed from a safe and loving father. Bill looked out for me like a good dad would.

I sent love to anyone who'd receive it—at the grocery store, the post office, on the street. This magnetic light knew no strangers. I'd smile at everyone and sometimes hug people with whom I'd had brief chats. I realized there were many people on my frequency, and there was no shortage of love.

All my addictions slipped away. I simply forgot about them, especially my need to have a relationship. I loved every moment of my life, even, surprisingly, the painful ones. I knew the uncomfortable feelings were a chance to change myself. During my spiritual quest, I'd heard that pain was like making gold in a cauldron—that suffering was burning off the impurities, leaving only refined gold. We could either avoid the process or embrace it. I was tired of the fearful, toxic thoughts that kept driving me into pain. I was genuinely ready to have them burned off and replaced with pure love.

♥

Once I stopped searching and focused on loving others,
love came to me.

My life was so complete and fulfilled that I didn't think about dating. So, I was taken aback when one of the guys in my recovery meetings asked me to go for coffee. When I ran it by Bill, he approved. We remained friends for many months. I wanted to see his true character and if we'd be compatible. We developed safety and trust in each other. For the first time, I heard things like "Oh good!" instead of "Oh God!" from my friends. We were married one year after our first date. I now enjoy the type of relationship that has been in my mind since I was five years old. A couple who can talk with each other, problem-solve with respect, have fun, enjoy family, and share a true partnership. Once I stopped searching and focused on loving others, love came to me. What I'd always wanted was now mine.

♥

A magic wand doesn't create miracles,
but miracles are magical.

The Right Path: It Starts and Ends with Self-Love

A magic wand doesn't create miracles, but miracles are magical.

The path of love was so much easier than the path of fear. I'd been split between the two my whole life. Like so many of us, I had missed the entire point of life. I was under the illusion that if I did all the right things, I could make things happen. Not so with love. When I learned to love myself the way I wanted to be loved, love found itself, and fear in all its disguises lost its power over me.

❤

Your part on this planet is as essential as anyone else's.
Don't allow fear to rob you of your destiny, your future,
and your life's purpose. You deserve to be happy.

My story isn't unique, and many heroes and heroines have overcome far greater trials. I want you to see that it doesn't matter how many mistakes you've made or how badly you feel about yourself or what horrible things have happened to you; you can still turn those messes into miracles and use those experiences to help others.

The seventh path is the most important because it encompasses all the other paths. Your part on this planet is as essential as anyone else's. Don't allow fear to rob you of your destiny, your future, and your life's purpose. You deserve to be happy.

❤

You always have a choice between the two voices
of love or fear.

You always have a choice between the two voices of love or fear. Fear will keep you stuck. Love will free you. Fear is living in anger and guilt. Love is living in peace and harmony. Fear means honoring resentment. Love is embracing freedom from bondage. Fear is trudging through life. Love is soaring on the wings of joy. Fear is living in hell, and love is heaven right now.

When all is said and done, do you want to look back on your life with satisfaction or wish you'd never been born? You were born for a reason— have you embraced that mission?

♥

You were born for a reason—
have you embraced that mission?

Are you ready to share and receive true love? Have you replaced loving relationships with material objects? There's nothing wrong with nice things, and an abundant life is a good thing when you are sharing with others. But possessions can't hug, comfort, and love you. True love is when you go into each day radiating your light without walls and you recognize your brothers and sisters are all around you. You are never alone. Love is forgiveness and grace. It's staying connected to your gifts that manifest into your mission and purpose on this heavenly planet. It's refusing to see limitations and lack in yourself and others, while fulfilling your mission by using your God-given gifts and talents. It's staying connected to the most important guidance you will ever receive—deep within yourself.

The voice of love is your guide. Almost every day, I hear of a miracle from someone who finds this voice. Just recently, a dear woman told me she was thinking of what to order for her next meal when she heard the voice of love say, "Are you going to wait another twenty years to lose that twenty pounds you've been trying to lose for the past twenty years?" She was love-stuck and took in the message. Over the next few months, she lost weight, but even more important, she felt love for herself instead of powerlessness and contempt. Once she replaced food with self-love, she exuded the joy of her healing moment.

When you love yourself, there's no more need for false substitutes. You no longer confuse loving something with loving yourself. You recognize the value of a healthy body and a clear mind, and you won't violate these precious resources. You know they won't last forever, but you tenderly care for them in ways that are uplifting and not destructive. And when bad things happen, you use them to transform messes into miracles so that you can evolve into all you were meant to be. As you become more connected to the voice of love, you know that comfort and guidance are always present. That voice can provide a solution to any problem. You are never alone.

♥

**There's no time better than right now to
learn to love yourself.**

Remember, there's a path that can turn every mess into a miracle. You are here to share and receive love, and that's the most important path of all. There's no time better than right now to learn to love yourself.

To have love, be the love that you want.

Your Healing Moment Exercise 7:
Finding Self-Love

You are the most important person you will ever love, and everything is a reflection of that self-love. The following exercises can help you to pinpoint the blocks that have prevented you from obtaining love and identify how to find it.

1. What are some of the ways you've tried to find love?

   _____

   _____

2. Have you confused using something that makes you feel good with something that makes you feel good about yourself? If so, what are some of your substitutes for love?

   _____

   _____

   _____

3. What are some loving actions that you could add to your daily life that would help the seeds of love grow? For example, replacing an unloving behavior with a healthy one.

_____

_____

_____

4. List one thing that you will replace. For example, replace some television time with reading, isolating with helping someone, snacking with going for a walk, boredom with a new hobby or interest, etc.

_____

_____

_____

5. What is your purpose here? How will you fulfill that purpose?

_____

_____

_____

6. Who is the most important person you will ever love? How will you get the love you want?

_____

_____

_____

7. Why are you here? What are your talents? How have you turned your misfortunes into your mission?

_____

_____

_____

Three-Step Exercise for Self-Love

1. Close your eyes and visualize your birth.
2. Tell that beautiful baby the love you feel.
3. See yourself holding that baby and feeling pure love for that precious infant. Tell that infant how special they are and what great things they will achieve.

CONCLUSION

My deepest desire is that we humans will find our way back to our birth-right of happiness and joy.

I wrote this book for those who haven't been able to achieve this God-given, natural state. I don't want you to suffer through years of searching like I did. While those decades weren't wasted, I spent a lot of time and money largely on disappointment. I have no regrets, as each misstep was a step toward this moment, but I hope these seven paths help you see your light and save you unnecessary costs to your body, wallet, and soul.

Some people won't find their healing moment; some will. It is always available. Those who are open and committed will, and those who close their hearts and minds won't.

Just the other day, I heard a speaker who had unknowingly used these seven paths to turn his disastrous life into a miraculous one. A teen drug addict turned hardened criminal, he had been in and out of prison forty-five times and had gone to more than fifteen treatment centers. But finally, he reached the point where he asked God for help and listened to his *inner guidance* (first path), and then nothing was ever the same. He had a spiritual awakening and a psychic change and learned to control himself rather than allowing drugs and crime to *control him* (second path). Even though he was a year sober, he had to serve in the federal penitentiary for previous crimes, but he knew he could *trust* himself to make the right choices when tempted (third path). He was disturbed by his past behaviors but made amends to people he'd hurt and knew if he didn't *forgive* himself and others, he'd threaten his recovery (fourth path). In prison, he gained *respect* (fifth path) for himself and others by holding twelve-step meetings and helping other people stay sober and become spiritually fit. When he was released from prison, he started his own trade business. Ten years later and *prosperous* (sixth path), he has fifty employees, one of them a one-time competitor whose business he bought and whom he hired as a manager. About that time, he met a woman who was also in recovery but had lost custody of her two children. They supported each other's recovery. He helped her get her children back. They married and gave birth to two additional children. They share their story whenever called upon to do so. They are the *love* that they want (seventh path). This is how miracles work. No magic: just a commitment to choose love over fear and to do the next loving thing brought forth the happiness he had sought his entire life.

You are responsible for yourself. You can delegate that responsibility to other people or deities, but no person or thing will take better care of you than yourself. By embracing this truth, you can reclaim your power and then collaborate with all that the universe offers to achieve your goals. So, practice the seven paths, whether you feel like it or not, and always remember that love is an action word, not a thing or a state of being.

You are not here to suffer. You are here on this magical playground only to experience a magnificent journey. Like any magic kingdom, it has its glories, hardships, and mysteries. The planet you're on will not change, but your perception of what's possible here can.

A Course in Miracles reminds us, "Love waits on welcome, not on time."[1] In other words, you're not waiting on love; love is waiting for you to invite it into your heart and mind. By tapping into the greatest resource of all—the love within—you can fulfill your life's purpose: to share and receive love.

I hope that you will apply these seven paths to your life. I know that they can do for you what they did for me. When we redirect our energy to being the change that we want to see, we can find the peace and joy we seek to live in. And after we've reached that state, we can help others find their way here to join us.

Love is yours. Love is your inheritance. Love is your birthright. Claim it, feel it, be it. There's no better time than now. You need only join in and follow your path to the miracles of love.

ACKNOWLEDGMENTS

Thank you to all my teachers—the good ones and the bad. Special thanks to my mom for excavating the spiritual roots with which I was born.

Thanks to my friend Mary Lydon—this book would not have been published without her introduction to an agent. To my agent Devra Jacobs, who found the perfect publishing platform for a wandering writer. To Michele Ashriani Cohn and Richard Cohn, for their faith in publishing this book. To the editors; Bailey Potter, Lindsay Easterbrooks-Brown, Emmalisa Sparrow Wood, Kristin Thiel, and Sarah Heilman for their editorial expertise. And especially to the Universe for magically bringing us all together.

Gratitude to everyone who ever helped me when I couldn't get up anymore. Special thanks to all the antagonists from whom I learned the power of forgiveness. I am who I am because of these teachers.

APPENDIX

77 Ways to Self-Love

Here are some suggestions that I have developed over the course of my life and now wish to share with you in your journey to self-love. Browse and pick a few to incorporate into your day. There's no reason to rush or make this a project. It's not work—it's the path to love.

1. Be grateful for the pillow, blanket, and sheets, and cuddle up.
2. Make your bed (with a smile).
3. Be grateful for toothpaste and water.
4. Enjoy the first beverage of the day—smell the aroma and be grateful for the cup.
5. Read a book you've always wanted to read.
6. Look all around you, focusing on how creation has manifested everything you see and made your life more pleasant—everything we take for granted.
7. Eat healthy food for breakfast with an appreciation for its source.

♥   ♥   ♥   ♥   ♥   ♥   ♥

8. Wash your dishes with gratitude for having dishes to eat from.
9. Exercise, even if only for fifteen minutes (like a walk).

10. Enjoy the soap and water when you bathe, being grateful you have access to them.
11. Tell someone you love them.
12. Tell someone what you appreciate about them.
13. Do a favor for someone else.
14. Listen to music that you love.

♥   ♥   ♥   ♥   ♥   ♥   ♥

15. Reach out to check on someone.
16. Spend five minutes looking at something beautiful.
17. When your fear-based mind says, "I don't like this," try saying, "I do like this. There's an opportunity for a miracle here."
18. Embrace all feelings—sink into them until they pass; do not act on them until they die.
19. Don't act on any feelings until you embrace the fear underneath.
20. Listen to the loving voice inside of you and learn to trust it.
21. Make a vision board and keep adding to it.

♥   ♥   ♥   ♥   ♥   ♥   ♥

22. Speak the truth—in a loving way.
23. Get a massage.
24. Pay bills on time.
25. Watch your favorite movie.
26. Meditate, even for a few minutes.
27. Volunteer.
28. Treat yourself to a nice meal out (it doesn't have to be expensive).

♥   ♥   ♥   ♥   ♥   ♥   ♥

29. Buy a cookbook or a recipe app—learn a new recipe every week.
30. When you react, sit alone with the feeling—let it out.
31. Go to recovery meetings.
32. Smell fresh flowers.

33. Gaze into the stars.
34. Watch a comedy.
35. Refuse to listen to the internal saboteur that tells you to "do it later." Do it now.

♥   ♥   ♥   ♥   ♥   ♥   ♥

36. Make a bucket list.
37. Eat a healthy lunch.
38. Detach with love from a situation that doesn't feel good.
39. Make your home as cozy as possible.
40. Say thank you every time someone compliments you.
41. Get an organizer and get organized.
42. Ignore the addict's chatter telling you to use.

♥   ♥   ♥   ♥   ♥   ♥   ♥

43. Give yourself three compliments a day.
44. Journal.
45. Smile at yourself in the mirror.
46. Forgive yourself.
47. Cry when you're sad.
48. Once you've healed it, refuse to dwell on the past.
49. Listen to a self-help podcast.

♥   ♥   ♥   ♥   ♥   ♥   ♥

50. Identify the fear under your guilt.
51. Identify the fear under anger.
52. Move through the fear.
53. Take a fifteen-minute power nap.
54. Call a relative.
55. Refuse to cave in to shame; hold your head up high.
56. Remind yourself, "I'm safe right now."

♥ ♥ ♥ ♥ ♥ ♥ ♥

57. Spend five-plus minutes with nature.
58. Scream into a pillow.
59. Get a medical or dental checkup.
60. Go to the barbershop or hair salon.
61. Stick to facts.
62. Complete therapy assignments.
63. When you feel needy, do something for someone else.

♥ ♥ ♥ ♥ ♥ ♥ ♥

64. Acknowledge your mistakes—to yourself and others.
65. Listen to the sounds of silence.
66. Make a habit of saying, "I am currently responsible for my life. Me."
67. Become comfortable with waiting, and make time for yourself.
68. If you make a mistake, clean it up; don't keep pulling it out of the garbage can.
69. Start a conversation with a friendly neighbor.
70. Finish one project before moving on to the next.

♥ ♥ ♥ ♥ ♥ ♥ ♥

71. Keep your commitment or negotiate a better one.
72. Thank your higher power for something before you get into bed at night.
73. Tell your kids or other younger people important in your life something you appreciate about them.
74. Tell yourself the truth.
75. List three things you're proud of.
76. Be grateful for the weather (sunny or stormy)—Mother Earth needs all.
77. Share a favorite story.

♥   ♥   ♥   ♥   ♥   ♥   ♥

You can keep adding your own! And remember, you have two voices in your head—listen to the voice of love.

NOTES

Introduction

1. Demush Bajrami, Arburim Iseni, and Anesa Topko, "Subversion—The Secret Power of the Message Enlaced with the Power of the Internet and Information Technology," *Khazar Journal of Humanities and Social Sciences* 22, no. 3 (2019): 60 70, https://doi.org/10.5782/2223-2621.2019.22.3.60.
2. "11 Examples of Advertising and Marketing with Subliminal Messages," MDirector, January 18, 2017, https://www.mdirector.com/en/digital-marketing/examples-marketing-subliminal-messages.html.
3. "Cardiovascular Diseases," World Health Organization, accessed August 25, 2021, https://www.who.int/westernpacific/health-topics/cardiovascular-diseases.
4. Hannah Ritchie, "How Many People in the World Die from Cancer?" Our World in Data, February 1, 2021, https://ourworldindata.org/how-many-people-in-the-world-die-from-cancer.
5. Amanda Barrell, "Lung Diseases: What to Know," *Medical News Today*, April 28, 2021, https://www.medicalnewstoday.com/articles/types-of-lung-diseases.

6. Eric Donkor, "Stroke in the 21st Century: A Snapshot of the Burden, Epidemiology, and Quality of Life," Stroke Research and Treatment, November 27, 2018, https://doi.org/10.1155/2018/3238165.

7. "Diabetes," World Health Organization, November 10, 2021, https://www.who.int/news-room/fact-sheets/detail/diabetes.

8. "COVID-19 pandemic triggers 25% increase in prevalence of anxiety and depression worldwide," World Health Organization, March 2, 2022, https://www.who.int/news/item/02-03-2022-covid-19 -pandemic-triggers-25-increase-in-prevalence-of-anxiety-and -depression-worldwide.

9. Jamie Ducharme, "Watching War Unfold on Social Media Affects Your Mental Health," Time, March 8, 2022, https://time.com/6155630 /ukraine-war-social-media-mental-health/.

10. Hannah Ritchie, Max Roser, and Esteban Ortiz-Ospina, "Suicide," Our World Data, accessed May 13, 2022, https://ourworldindata .org/suicide.

11. "Total Number of People Taking Psychiatric Drugs in the United States | CCHR International," Citizens Commission on Human Rights International: The Mental Health Industry Watchdog, January 2021, https://www.cchrint.org/psychiatric-drugs/people -taking-psychiatric-drugs/.

12. "Mental Disorder Drugs Market Size Worth US$58.91 Billion by 2031," Visiongain Research, Inc., GlobeNewswire, June 11, 2021. https:// www.globenewswire.com/en/news-release/2021/06/11/2245922/0 /en/Mental-Disorder-Drugs-Market-size-worth-US-58-91-Billion -by-2031-Visiongain-Research-Inc.html.

13. Kelly Brogan, MD, and Kristin Loberg, A Mind of Your Own (London: Harper Thorsons, 2016).

14. "Part 1: The Connection Between Substance Use Disorders and Mental Illness," National Institute on Drug Abuse, April 13, 2021, https://www.drugabuse.gov/publications/research-reports/common -comorbidities-substance-use-disorders/part-1-connection-between -substance-use-disorders-mental-illness.

15. Joseph Detrano, "Sugar Addiction: More Serious Than You Think," Rutgers Center of Alcohol & Substance Use Studies, accessed

May 17, 2022, https://alcoholstudies.rutgers.edu/sugar-addiction
-more-serious-than-you-think/.

16. Anahad O'Connor, "Are Foods Labeled 'Low Sugar' Misleading Consumers?" *New York Times*, February 26, 2020, https://www.nytimes
.com/2020/02/26/well/eat/are-foods-labeled-low-sugar-misleading
-consumers.html.

17. Helen Shucman, *A Course in Miracles* (New York: Foundation for
Inner Peace, 1976), vii.

18. Shucman, vii, viii.

19. "Overview of *A Course in Miracles*," Miracle Distribution Center,
accessed May 9, 2022, https://www.miraclecenter.org/wp/about
/a-course-in-miracles/.

20. "Overview of *A Course in Miracles*."

21. An *Introduction to A Course in Miracles*, free PDF (Anaheim, CA:
Miracle Distribution Center, 1987), https://www.miraclecenter.org
/media/IntroductiontoACIM.pdf.

22. Shucman, 473.

Chapter 1

1. "November 19, 1978," *American Experience*, accessed May 13, 2022,
https://www.pbs.org/wgbh/americanexperience/features/jonestown
-nov-18-1978/.

2. Emily Zokbi, "The Catholic Church Has Paid Nearly $4 Billion
Over Sexual Abuse Claims, Group Says," *Newsweek*, August 25, 2018,
https://www.newsweek.com/over-3-billion-paid-lawsuits-catholic
-church-over-sex-abuse-claims-1090753.

3. Curtis Weyant, "Priests Accused of Sexual Abuse," Consumer Safety,
July 29, 2020, https://www.consumersafety.org/personal-injury
-lawsuits/catholic-church/accused-priests/.

4. Curtis Weyant, "Catholic Church Sexual Abuse Lawsuit," Consumer Safety, January 13, 2021, https://www.consumersafety.org
/personal-injury-lawsuits/catholic-church/.

5. Meagan Flynn, "Celebrity Brazilian Healer 'John of God,' Once Fea-
tured by Oprah, Surrenders on Sexual Abuse Charges," *Washington*

Post, December 17, 2018, https://www.washingtonpost.com
/nation/2018/12/17/celebrity-brazilian-healer-john-god-once
-featured-by-oprah-surrenders-sexual-abuse-charges/.
6. Kylie Wolfe, "Misuse of Anti-Anxiety Drugs Linked to Overdose
Deaths," *Headline Discoveries*, Spring/Summer 2019, https://www
.fishersci.com/us/en/education-products/publications/headline-dis
coveries/2019/spring-summer-issue/misuse-antianxiety-drugs
-linked-overdose-deaths.html.
7. "A Day to Remember—International Overdose Awareness Day,"
Centers for Disease Control and Prevention, accessed May 14,
2022, https://www.cdc.gov/drugoverdose/featured-topics/ioad-benzo
-overdose.html.
8. Donovan T. Maust, MD, A. Lin Lewel, MD, and Frederic C. Blow,
PhD, "Benzodiazepine Use and Misuse Among Adults in the United
States," *Psychiatry Services* 70, no. 2, (February 1, 2019): 97–106,
https://doi.org/10.1176/appi.ps.201800321.
9. Ashish Sarangi, Terry McMahon, Jayasudha Gude, "Benzodiazepine
Misuse: An Epidemic Within a Pandemic," *Cureus* 13, no. 6, (June
2021), https://doi.org/10.7759/cureus.15816.

Chapter 3

1. Carol Rao, "Was Michael Jordon Really Cut from His High School
Basketball Team?" Sports Casting, March 14, 2020, https://www
.sportscasting.com/was-michael-jordan-really-cut-from-his-high
-school-basketball-team/.
2. Camila Santiago, "Oprah Winfrey's Path to Success Included a Traumatic Childhood Riddled with Abuse from Relatives," Amo Mama,
September 28, 2021, https://news.amomama.com/279732-oprah
-winfreys-path-success-included-a-t.html.
3. Ryan Robinson, "How Steve Jobs Learned to Embrace Failure and
Saved Apple," The Balance Small Business, May 30, 2019, https://
www.thebalancesmb.com/steve-jobs-and-how-embracing-failure
-saved-apple-1200640.

4. Erin Blakemore, "Thomas Edison Didn't Invent the Lightbulb, but Here's What He Did Do," *National Geographic*, April 13, 2022. https://www.nationalgeographic.com/history/article/thomas-edison -light-bulb-history.

5. Dr. Howard Markel, "The Medical Mystery that Helped Make Thomas Edison an Inventor," *PBS Newshour*, October 22, 2018, https://www.pbs.org/newshour/health/the-medical-mystery -that-helped-make-thomas-edison-an-inventor.

6. Christopher Rosa and Samantha Leach, "12 Famous Women on Facing—and Overcoming—Failure," *Glamour*, January 29, 2019, https://www.glamour.com/story/famous-women-failure-quotes.

7. Eudie Pak, "Walt Disney's Rocky Road to Success," *Biography*, modified June 17, 2020, https://www.biography.com/news/walt -disney-failures.

8. James Asquith, "Did You Know Walt Disney Was Rejected 300 Times for Mickey Mouse and His Theme Park?" *Forbes*, December 29, 2019, https://www.forbes.com/sites/jamesasquith/2020/12/29 /did-you-know-walt-disney-was-rejected-300-times-for-mickey -mouse-and-his-theme-park/?sh=63dff6b04a97.

Chapter 4

1. Elisabeth Kübler-Ross, *On Death and Dying*, 50th anniversary ed. (New York: Scribner, 2014).

2. David Kessler, *Finding Meaning, The Sixth Stage of Grieving* (New York: Scribner, 2019).

Chapter 5

1. Shakespeare, *Hamlet*, Act 1, scene 3, lines 78–80, http://shakespeare .mit.edu/hamlet/full.html.

Chapter 6

1. Charles Dickens, *A Christmas Carol* (England: Chapman and Hall, 1873).
2. Napoleon Hill, *Think and Grow Rich* (New York: TarcherPerigee, 2005).

Chapter 7

1. Shucman, *A Course in Miracles*, 233.

Conclusion

1. Shucman, *A Course in Miracles*, 255.

About the Author

Dr. Donna Marks has been a licensed psychotherapist and addictions counselor in Palm Beach, Florida, for over thirty years. In 1989, Dr. Marks developed a chemical dependency training program at Palm Beach Community College, which has grown into a four-year degree and received an Award of Appreciation from the college and the Florida Governor's Council Award. She is also a certified gestalt therapist, psychoanalyst, hypnotist, and sex therapist. She teaches *A Course in Miracles*, along with sharing her methods with hundreds of thousands of listeners on podcasts and radio shows. Learn more about Dr. Marks, her books, and services at www.DrDonnaMarks.com.

Other Books by Dr. Donna Marks

Exit the Maze: One Addiction, One Cause, One Solution, an extended and revised edition (Beyond Words Publishing, 2022)

Exit the Maze: One Addiction, One Cause, One Cure (Westward Publishing, 2020)

Learn, Grow, Forgive: A Path to Spiritual Success (Balboa Press, 2019)

♥   ♥   ♥   ♥   ♥   ♥   ♥

If you have ever experienced your own healing moment, your miracle could help other people, so please visit www.DrDonnaMarks.com and share your story on my website.